SOLVING **CORRUPTION** IN THE CHURCH AND NATION

Richard J. Gehman

OASIS
INTERNATIONAL
PUBLISHING

Published by Oasis International Ltd. in partnership with Richard J. Gehman. Oasis International is a ministry devoted to growing discipleship through publishing African voices.

• We engage Africa's most influential, most relevant, and best communicators for the sake of the gospel.

• We cultivate local and global partnerships in order to publish and distribute high-quality books and Bibles.

• We create contextual content that meets the specific needs of Africa, has the power to transform individuals and societies, and gives the church in Africa a global voice.

Oasis is: Satisfying Africa's Thirst for God's Word. For more information, go to oasisinternational.com.

The author and publisher have made every effort to ensure that the information in this book was correct at press time and disclaim any liability to any party for any loss, damage, or disruption caused by errors or omissions, whether such errors or omissions result from negligence, accident, or any other cause. However, if you feel that your work was not accurately cited, please reach out to us at info@oasisinternational.com and we will make every effort to review and correct the book where required. Furthermore, any internet addresses (websites, blogs, etc.), telephone numbers, or the like in this book are offered only as a resource. They are not intended in any way to be or imply an endorsement by Oasis, nor does Oasis vouch for this content.

Printed in India

22 23 24 25 26 27 28 29 30 31 BPI 10 9 8 7 6 5 4 3 2 1

CONTENTS

FOREWORD

Dr. Jeremiah Mutie (Ph.D.), Professor of Theology and Church History in Southern California Seminary.

In *Solving Corruption in the Church and Nation*, Dr. Richard J. Gehman, long serving A.I.M. missionary to Africa, presents a compelling case study on the thorny question of the church-state relationships, focusing on the vice of corruption. Through numerous examples of news items that span over decades, corresponding to his stay and work in Kenya, Dr. Gehman argues that, with good discipleship practices, the church in Kenya is best placed to provide leadership to society in its attempt to deal with this crippling vice. However, as he argues, this is only possible if the church cleans her own backyard first. Gehman's work not only provides a blueprint for dealing with the vice of corruption, specifically in Kenya and Africa in general, but, by extension, it serves in the same capacity for believers everywhere in the world with Kenya serving as the case study. I, therefore, highly recommend it specifically to Christians in Kenya as well as others who are interested in dealing with corruption both in state and the church as well as discipleship in general.

Rev. Dr. James Mbuva (Ph.D.) Professor of Education in National University

Unfortunately, the church all too often seems to imitate the behavior of corruption in the nation. Instead of the church modeling Jesus Christ through loving justice and kindness, walking humbly before God, hating sin, shunning corruption and bribery, and all kinds of defrauding activities; and instead of reflecting the behavior and attitudes of faithfulness, diligence, honesty, and integrity of Jesus Christ, many church leaders fall into the corruptible patterns of the world. Finally, Dr. Richard Gehman, as a prolific leader, educator, and author, has adequately addressed corruption in the nation and the church and provided solutions. *Solving Corruption in the Church and Nation* is reader-friendly. It carefully addresses relevant issues eating the Church of Jesus Christ today, and provides the answers for building vibrant Christian churches.

Rev. Dr. Elias Ng'etich (Ph.D), Professor of Religious Studies in Moi University

Solving Corruption in the Church and Nation by Richard Gehman is not only a timely book, but a helpful tool for Christian churches because its proposed solution to corruption is biblical, relevant, and attainable. Though corruption is a global human menace, the Kenyan case study illustrated by the book, shows the devastating ravages of the vice in a particular context. Dr. Gehman meaningfully uses Kenya as a case study to illustrate the global nature of corruption and its impact. Using national newspaper clippings from the 1980s and 1990s, those reports astoundingly reflect Kenya's contemporary state. According to Kenya's Ethics and Anti-Corruption Commission (EACC), 7.8% of Kenya's GDP is lost to corruption annually. An urgent remedy is needed, hence my endorsement and recommendation of the book for all Christians and churches to study and implement.

ABBREVIATIONS FOR THE BOOKS OF THE BIBLE

Genesis	Ge	Isaiah	Isa	Romans	Ro
Exodus	Ex	Jeremiah	Jer	1 Corinthians	1 Co
Leviticus	Lev	Lamentations	La	2 Corinthians	2 Co
Numbers	Nu	Ezekiel	Eze	Galatians	Gal
Deuteronomy	Dt	Daniel	Da	Ephesians	Eph
Joshua	Jos	Hosea	Hos	Philippians	Php
Judges	Jdg	Joel	Joel	Colossians	Col
Ruth	Ru	Amos	Am	1 Thessalonians	1 Th
1 Samuel	1 Sa	Obadiah	Ob	2 Thessalonians	2 Th
2 Samuel	2 Sa	Jonah	Jnh	1 Timothy	1 Ti
1 Kings	1 Ki	Micah	Mic	2 Timothy	2 Ti
2 Kings	2 Ki	Nahum	Na	Titus	Tit
1 Chronicles	1 Ch	Habakkuk	Hab	Philemon	Phm
2 Chronicles	2 Ch	Zephaniah	Zep	Hebrews	Heb
Ezra	Ezr	Haggai	Hag	James	Jas
Nehemiah	Ne	Zechariah	Zec	1 Peter	1 Pe
Esther	Est	Malachi	Mal	2 Peter	2 Pe
Job	Job	Matthew	Mt	1 John	1 Jn
Psalms	Ps	Mark	Mk	2 John	2 Jn
Proverbs	Pr	Luke	Lk	3 John	3 Jn
Ecclesiastes	Ecc	John	Jn	Jude	Jude
Song of Solomon	SS	Acts	Ac	Revelation	Rev

PREFACE

During our thirty-six years of life and service in Kenya (1966-2002), I read the daily newspaper religiously, especially the Daily Nation. I loved it. During our Home Assignments I would tell my American friends that I valued the Kenyan newspapers far more than the American publications. The Kenya newspapers reflected life in Kenya, the good and the bad.

We read of national triumphs and crises. The sudden death of the Mzee, President Jomo Kenyatta, stunned the nation, followed by the peaceful transition of Daniel Arap Moi as the second president of Kenya. We read of the numerous athletic triumphs of Kenyan heroes like Kipchoge Keino, Daniel Komen, Paul Tergat, Moses Kiptanui and Richard Chelimo. The world famous East Africa Safari gripped everyone living in this geographically diverse nation as we watched in person this fascinating car race, tracking the serpentine, rugged roads of Kenya.

The fascinating accounts of African traditional culture captivated the national readership. As one headline said: "Which traditions do we keep?" The frequent burial disputes over famous people like S.M. Otieno, Jaramogi Odinga and Robert Wangila provided many weeks and months of fascinating reading. The female circumcision controversy which ripped apart the Christian churches in the 1930s still continued into the 1990s as the government tried to ban the practice of "female mutilation."

Discussing traditional rites of circumcision the editors asked, "Is the sun setting on a cherished tradition?" "Is [bride-price] an outmoded or still essential tradition?" All kinds of issues were discussed: forced marriages, polygamy, wife-inheritance, inheritance laws, witchcraft, and black magic. A headline read: "Does the African culture shut out modernization?" Philip Ochieng answered: "Laying to rest a number of outmoded cultural practices."

The courageous Kenyan journalists also narrated the complexities of Kenyan society: the social ills, cultural challenges, political intrigues and every imaginable aspect of Kenya.

I must admit that the inauguration of the multiparty system of politics in 1992 stole some of the luster for me because the newspapers became obsessed with the conflicts and power struggles between the different political parties and politicians. Nevertheless, Kenyan newspapers continued to be essential reading.

So fascinated was I with the newspaper reports that I began clipping articles of interest, especially during the 1980s and 1990s. When returning to the United States in 2002 for retirement, we freighted home a box filled with newspaper clippings measuring a cubic 15 inches (38 centimeters). This box set in our garage for seventeen years waiting for my attention.

As I eventually began sorting through these clippings and collating them into different categories, I was stirred with admiration once again by the courageous professionalism of these Kenyan journalists and editors who are the equals of their colleagues in the West by any standard.

One aspect of our lives in Kenya was the privilege of becoming bosom friends of many Kenyans, mostly the students and graduates of Scott Theological College where we taught. In fact, I came to be and feel closer to many of these male Kenyans than with any of my American friends.

During this process of making friendship I discovered a fascinating truth which is known by everyone with cross-cultural friendships. Once you get beneath the skin color and racial characteristics, and once you navigate the frustrating differences of cultural values, you discover a common humanity. Not only do blood types defy any racial distinctions, human nature is the same. Human beings, whether white, black or brown, are all descended from one human parent, Adam and Eve. We are all made in the image of God and all deeply flawed through the sinful nature inherited from Adam and Eve.

Chicken eggs are so similar to human beings. They come in different colors – white, tan, speckled – and yet when you open them up, they are the same inside. Racial and cultural differences are what you see on the outside, but inside you find one human race, all made in the image of God and all flawed by sin and needing the grace of God for salvation.

This book is derived from reflections on these Kenyan newspaper clipping, but they point to moral and spiritual issues that are universal. This will be made clear as we identify similar problems in the United States as those found in Kenya. Likewise, the solution for these social ills in Kenya apply equally to the many social issues in America.

Therefore, let it be known and understood, that this book is not pointing to Kenya's social ills as if they were aberrant or uniquely African. The old adage is true. When you point your index finger at someone with blame, you have three fingers pointing back on the one entering into judgment.

The greatest of all virtues is humility. If we can all admit that we are one humanity and suffer from the same temptations and are guilty of the same crimes, the easier it will be to accept one another, love one another and forgive one another. With this in mind we now focus on the purpose of this book.

Kenya, like all other nations in this world, is troubled by many social ills. As evangelical Christians we believe the solution is the gospel of Jesus Christ. Through faith in Christ people are converted and baptized into the Body of Christ, the invisible Church universal. They become members of a visible local congregation of believers.

Through the evangelizing and discipling ministry of the Church more and more are converted. Together they form the visible church and are mandated by Christ to be salt and light in society: *salt* to preserve society from moral filth, and *light* to show the path to godly living through faith and obedience to Jesus Christ.

The major problem is that in practice the Christian Church so often reflects the same moral rot found in society. The Church has failed to be salt and light.

The purpose of this book is to shine light on this problem and explore a biblical solution. If you are sick and tired of the corruption in society – and in the church – this book is for you because it points to the solution for this ongoing and unending moral mess.

1

SOCIAL ILLS

Societal problems are complex and cannot be reduced to simple diagnoses and solutions. Further, social ills are only symptoms of deeper problems. Underlying the visible problems are root causes. We will explore the underlying ills of social ills under four headings: *egotism, lust, greed and apathy*. In actual fact, all root causes can be traced back to one fatal flaw in human nature: egotism/pride, a desire to exalt self and live autonomously apart from God and his will.

EGOTISM

Pride is one of seven cardinal sins that have plagued the human race from the beginning. Pride says "I want to be the first, the best, and the greatest. I want to be the leader. I will prevail over all others." In brief, this is egotism – me first.

The problem is that most people are unaware of their pride. Proud people exalt themselves over others, feeling they are better than others. Pride leads to power struggles, prejudice, hatred and violence. Kenya and all the nations of the world are embroiled in this problem of egotism.

Power Struggles

The big ego in every human heart leads to power struggles at every level. In the cultural traditions of many African communities, "the Big Man" is the prototype of leadership. Although the king or traditional chief may consult with the elders, his word was final. No one dared to oppose him.

In order to remain in power in modern times a leader must maintain the loyalty of his people, either through bribes or through force. By any means necessary leaders have remained in power by changing the constitution or by fraudulently winning the elections or coalescing support through backroom, underhanded deals.

Kenya has experienced these same deadly power struggles of men trying to gain or retain their powerful positions. They cheat and steal and engage in corrupt deals, like several high-ranking Kenyan officials who were given fifty acre plots in the city of Nairobi, carved from Nairobi's City Park.

As one women who lived in the Nairobi slums told me, "The big fish eat up the little fish." Leadership corruption is rampant. Those in power are obsessed with property accumulation. The Big Shots seize land occupied by the little people. Big Shots get away with their crimes while the common man pays his full debt to society.

This is not a uniquely African problem. In western nations, which have had the advantage of hundreds of years of democracy and fifteen hundred years of Christianity, people game the system by using underhanded ways to win office and when in office, they mysteriously become wealthy although their official salaries are relatively small.

Prejudice

Prejudice is rooted in pride which elevates self over others. Prejudice is a preconceived opinion of others based on their religious affiliation, race, ethnic identity, education or social class. Prejudice prejudges others by putting others down in order to elevate one's ego.

Tribalism: One of the greatest social ills in Kenya and in all of Africa is tribalism. No one can deny this. Tribalism is the basis for hatred and conflict between the 1,000 ethnic communities in Africa. It is the greatest threat to unity within every African nation and the major cause for tearing nations apart. Each tribe seeks supremacy over others to gain material advantage. The Kenyan newspapers warned: "Tribalism is destroying Kenya," and "Tribalism is Kenya's greatest threat."

The more powerful and influential communities take advantage of the smaller and weaker ones. Tribalism is behind most land problems in Kenya. The British colonialists expropriated land claimed by Africans, herding them onto less desirable parcels so that white settlers could benefit. During the administration of the first Kenyan president this unjust land acquisition was only partially reversed. Instead, the Jomo Kenyatta administration favored the Gikuyu who prospered. Critics in turn felt the Kalenjin profited unduly during the rule of President Daniel Arap Moi. Politicians promote tribalism for political gain.

The Luo suffered the most because of tribalism. They alone among the ethnic communities of Kenya do not circumcise their young men and women during initiation. They are not Bantu but Nilotic. Therefore, they are looked down upon. Nandi Christian friends of mine, living in the highlands overlooking the Lake Basin where the Luo live, told me it was common to compare them with the uncircumcised Philistines.

Each ethnic community has its grievances, feeling slandered and neglected. They crave for respect and dignity. Prejudice leading to discrimination has caused every Kenyan community to yearn for dignity and acceptance.

Racism: The American ambassador to Kenya exhorted Kenyans to desist from tribal prejudice. Tribal hatred worried Ms Brazeal. From the Kenyan point of view this condescending moralizing required huge amounts of gall, given the rampant racism throughout America's history. It began with the enslavement of Africans and treating them as personal property. Even after the Civil War and the emancipation of the blacks, the Jim Crow laws followed which segregated public schools, public places, public transportation, restrooms, restaurants, and drinking fountains for whites and blacks.

Though much has been done to rectify legal injustices of the past, even electing the first African-American president, racial prejudice persists to this day among many Americans. Africa is tormented by tribalism and America is troubled by racism.

Is tribalism worse than racism? Is racism worse than tribalism? Is clannism less evil than tribalism? It all depends on your perspective. The naked truth is that they are all cut from the same cloth. Racism, tribalism, clannism and nationalism all are rooted in pride, egotism, self-centeredness and feeling superior to others. They all lead to the dehumanizing of all those whom they deem inferior. Both tribalism and racism are equally sinful and detestable before God.

Violence

A proud, self-centered, egotistical person slanders and displays prejudice. As hateful emotions are aroused, the violent slurs ultimately turn to physical violence. In a split second hatred becomes deadly and lifeless bodies lie scattered on the ground.

Violence occurs for various reasons. Cattle rustling, domestic disputes, clan tensions, land rows and revenge killings are common. Chaos erupted at City Hall between two councilors. Bandits beheaded ten people. Thieves terrorized a city hotel leaving two dead. Gangs invaded a home, stole valuables and injured the daughter. Angry mobs lynched three suspected thieves. Threats of armed violence were uttered if reform laws were not passed. Teachers and government ministers received death threats. Bandits attacked and robbed bus travelers on the Lamu-Mombasa road. Armed gangsters injured people during a shop raid. A priest was shot and killed when a gang stole his vehicle on the Nairobi-Nakuru road. A government minister was beaten, stoned and ejected from a burial ceremony. A street boy was beaten to death for stealing one sweet. University students rioted, burned cars, and destroyed property in protest over the introduction of part-time courses in medicine. Houses and churches were torched. People were displaced and became internal refugees.

In addition to these isolated incidences, Kenya has had her share of mass killings, most of them centered on ethnic divisions and land disputes. Ending the colonial rule, the Mau Mau slaughter arose over the many African grievances. A major injustice that riled the Kikuyu was the land taken from them and given to the white settlers. After four years of the declared Emergency, 2,000 Christian and pro-British Africans, 32 settlers, 90 white policemen and approximately 15,000 Mau Mau fighters had been killed.

Thirteen years later another oathing crisis arose. It all began on July 5, 1969, when Tom Mboya, a bright, promising, well-educated Luo leader, was assassinated because he was a threat to leadership. Immediately thereafter reports of oathing began to appear in the newspapers, a crisis which shook this young nation to its foundation.

During the following two decades Kenya had relative political peace under the strong leadership of Presidents Kenyatta and Moi with a *de facto* one party rule. Because the Kenya government was led by the heavy hand of Presidents Kenyatta and Moi, there were no massive violent conflicts, although ongoing skirmishes and fights broke out over grievances between the various ethnic groups and competing leadership. Prominent political figures like Joseph Kariuki and Robert Ouko were mysteriously assassinated with massive unrest following. But the united armed government kept the lid on the broiling emotions.

This relative peace and stability changed in 1992 when the multiparty system was introduced to Kenya under both internal and external pressure. President Moi succeeded in winning the elections in 1992 and 1997, though serious violence erupted before and after each election.

In 1992, before and after the national elections, violence killed 5,000 and displaced 250,000. The fighting occurred mostly in the Rift Valley Province with the epicenter in Molo though not limited to Molo. The hostilities were largely between the Kalenjin and the Kikuyu over the issue of land and political control.

The same outbreak of violence occurred in Kenya before and after the 1997 elections. Another 104 were killed and 10,000 victims displaced.

Such violence during national elections is unheard of in western countries, though violence for other reasons is common. Chicago is a violent city in America with 530 people killed in 2018, mostly gang related. In 2018 a total of 17,000 Americans were killed through gun violence, half of them by blacks killing blacks, mostly related to gangs fighting over drug issues in the inner cities. A mob of ten in Francisco punched, kicked and stoned to death a young Kenyan in San Francisco. Violence is universal in all nations, among all races and for many reasons, beginning with Cain killing his brother, Abel, out of jealousy.

GREED

Another pernicious root cause of social ills is greed. Lusting for things which do not belong to oneself leads to all kinds of dishonesty. We distinguish between egotism and greed, but in reality both are inter-related. A proud person is envious of others who have what he does not have. Egotism leads the greedy person to steal, and ultimately, to engage in violence.

Corruption

Dishonest practices for personal gain is what we call "corruption," an evil that is endemic in all nations including Kenya.

Land Grabbing: Land issues are a major problem in Kenya. Plots of land are grabbed from individuals, schools, churches, hospitals, city parks, *Jua Kali* entrepreneurs, and national forests. Irregular land allocations are made to developers and taken from public roads, privately owned farms, and even the Moi International Sports Arena. The list goes on and on.

Politically connected individuals use their position to pressure moneyed entities like the National Social Security Fund and banks to purchase worthless plots at exorbitant prices.

Land, given to a school by a presidential directive in 1989, was snatched by developers. Plots of land in Embu town, set aside for recreation, were illegally allocated to influential people.

Bribery: Bribery has become a pandemic scandal in Kenya. Bribery impoverishes citizens and kills industry which must add 30% for bribes to their production costs. Businesses cannot survive under this burden.

Matatu drivers frequently pay policemen bribes (*"chai"*) to overlook something illegal – a defective vehicle, overloading the vehicle, or lacking proper licenses or papers. Bribes are demanded in government offices for services that should be rendered freely. Bribes are expected by customs officers before one can receive the goods sent.

Theft

Stealing property from defenseless people takes many forms.

Cattle Rustlers: Cattle rustling by pastoralists is common. Hundreds of cattle and goats are stolen. Recovering them often leads to violent conflict.

Famine Food Sold: What was intended to feed starving people, who were suffering from famine, was sold for personal gain – a dastardly act!

Security Guards: To protect property in the cities, citizens hire security guards who are either useless (sleeping at night) or unscrupulous for they collude with thieves.

Highway Robberies: Kenyan roads, especially after dark, can be dangerous. Road blocks may be set up by thieves to stop vehicles who then forcefully rob the occupants of their valuables, sometimes even carjacking the vehicle, leaving the occupants battered and bruised by the roadside. Or the thieves suddenly appear on the road at night and stop the car at gunpoint to rob or kidnap the victims.

Feuding over Inheritance: When someone dies, family members sometimes feud among themselves over who should inherit the bequest. Greed is the motivator.

Disappearance of Imported Goods: Imported drugs worth millions of shillings disappeared. Hundreds of used imparted cars vanished overnight.

Dishonest Labor: Lazy workers who do not give an honest day's work are actually stealing from their employers. Stealing includes laziness, failing to provide an honest day's labor for a salary.

Petty Stealing: Luggage is taken by dishonest workers at the airport who claim the luggage is lost. Thieves in the city jiggle the car lock and take valuables from inside. Crooks, who posed as women in labor, managed to gain entrance into the maternity ward of a hospital and stole an incubator. During chaotic riots and civil disorder mobs looted and stole from stores.

A man managed to make a phone call from a public phone booth without paying money. Observers quickly notified the police who came and apprehended the thief. But a few minutes later the thief cheerfully returned, claiming he had bribed the police.

Ecological Theft: Indigenous hardwood trees have graced the slopes of Mt. Kenya, storing water and reducing climate change. But large swaths of forest have been denuded in order to plant large bhang plantations. Felled tree stumps are concealed from aerial view by covering them with elephant dung.

Cheating

Cheating is another form of stealing. People take all kinds of measures to gain unfair advantage over others.

Cheating in Exams: Cheating in universities was "rampant" according to news reports. With poor exam supervision students "dub" the answers, copying from their notes or small scraps of paper with tiny handwriting, or copy from another student's examination. One student estimated that 90% of students in her university cheated on exams. The stakes are so high that they justify dubbing. One is a fool who does not do it, she said.

This is not limited to varsities, but includes secondary school students. Even Alliance Boys High School, the premier high school with a stellar reputation, was knocked off the ranking list of high schools because of cheating by some students. Demands were made of the Kenya National Examinations Council to explain how the examination questions were leaked to certain students.

Cheating in Sports: The trickery of sportsmen using performance enhancing drugs is common in the west and has seeped into Kenyan sports as well.

LUST

An underlying cause of a grievous social ill is lust, that strong sexual drive in all humans. Kenya is not an island, isolated from the world. The world has become a global village where Kenya is interconnected with all other nations. The immoral values outside of the country are brought into this nation through the internet, literature, movies, tourism and the Kenyan university professors who studied overseas and learned immoral sexual mores while studying abroad. This external influence feeds into the fallen human nature of all Kenyans.

Sexual Promiscuity

Reports were made of indiscriminate sex on the rise with lose morals. Sexual promiscuity is destroying the sanctity of sex and marriage. Engaged couples engage in intimate intercourse _before_ their wedding vows. In one case a Catholic priest hastily married a couple because the bride was experiencing labor pains while waiting to take her wedding vows.

Male school teachers seduce their students by promising them good grades or threatening them with low grades if they do not yield to their sexual ultimatums. Students with weak grades submit to their lecturer's demands. Others find it desirable to drop a particular course or even leave the institution in order to avoid being trapped into immoral behavior.

It can be dangerous for adolescent schoolgirls to travel by _matatu_ because touts often lure them into immoral activities.

Nearly half of the single mothers in urban centers are the result of out-of-wedlock births. Children are born into this world without a father and mother rearing them, leaving the children to suffer grievously in poverty, illiteracy and exposed to immoral sexual behavior.

Homosexuality and Sex Change

During the 1980s and 1990s little was reported in the Kenyan newspapers about homosexuality and sex change.

In the second decade of the 21st century America is imploding as a result of the sexual revolution which took place in the 1960s. A total reversion of morality has taken place in America where homosexuality is rampant and gay marriages are now legal. What was considered immoral forever in the past is now both legalized and considered the only politically correct view. Anyone today who publicly voices opposition to homosexuality in America is accused of "hate speech" and "homophobia" and is subject to public ostracism.

Some American states and municipalities no longer register the gender of a child born. Gender remains an open question until the child decides for himself. It could be LGBTQ+. Crazy? It is beyond crazy. Having discarded the Judeo-Christian worldview and rejected God in the public sphere, the American elite and influence makers have lost their sanity.

Kenya is not isolated from the world and the perversions of the West seep into Africa through many means.

Two individuals were drinking at a local bar along the Kenyan coast. One person had curled hair, spoke with a soft, female-like voice and wore a dress. The other man was attracted to his new found friend wearing a dress. "She" had a flat chest so he assumed that "she" was a young woman. The two left the bar and walked arm in arm to a local lodging house. But when the two undressed inside, the male courter discovered his new found lover was actually a man. He began fighting with him and they both were arrested and taken to court which was perplexed. God save Kenya from the perversions emanating from the West!

Homosexuality, traditionally alien from most indigenous African peoples, is also being introduced with Kenyan male prostitutes offering their services to men in competition with the female prostitutes. A growing number of Kenyan youth consider homosexuality a romantic, high class trait, something they have obviously not learned from traditional Africans.

Prostitution

Prostitutes, otherwise known in politically correct society as sex workers, can be found in cities, along the coast among tourists, and conveniently located at truck stops. What has brought this scourge to international attention is the HIV plague which leads to Aids. A study found that 30% of truck drivers in Kenya had HIV infection, an indication of how sexually promiscuous truck drivers are.

Young, unemployed and uneducated youth are vulnerable to the lure of prostitution. Half of those beginning Standard One complete Primary School. Most who drop out are girls. Without a family support system and facing poverty, the sex trade is attractive.

As twilight settled on the town of Eldoret, heavily-perfumed and attractively dressed women could be seen on the streets heading for the bars and night clubs where men were drinking, smoking, flirting and looking for some sensual excitement.

The socially approved way of handling sexual promiscuity is not to urge faithfulness in marriage or to warn against the sin of fornication, but to accommodate the sexual drive of humans. Far from advocating purity, they urge protection from Aids by using condoms. Casual sex without condoms is condemned, not the act of adultery and fornication.

International drug trafficking syndicates are thought to be behind the child prostitution along the Kenya coast. Poverty is said to be the prime motivation for the child prostitutes who yearn for a few shillings, but behind them are big men who make huge profits. Pubs and night clubs where beer is consumed in great quantities are the places where prostitutes can be found. Barmaids, working where alcohol flows profusely, are often trapped in exploitation and immoral behavior.

Kenya is actually listed as the seventh biggest sex destination in the world. Male tourists visit Kenya's coast for the main purpose of fulfilling their sensual fantasies. A foreign born husband and wife arrived in Kenya together and then separated, each lusting after some beach boy or beach girl. Kenyan youth, yearning for monetary wealth, sell their bodies for a few hundred shillings.

One foreigner, without legal immigration documents, lived in a guest house for several years along Kenya's coast. He paid a primary school girl 500/sh. to have sex with him. In turn she lured other Primary School girls to cash in on this bonanza of 500/sh. for a one night adventure.

Rape

The uncontrolled sexual drive leads men to treat women as objects in order to satisfy their sensual passions. In 1994 the Kenya Commissioner of Police reported that within four years, 1989-1992, 1,600 women were raped. We may assume this number is a fraction of the actual number of rapes that took place.

Girls in boarding schools are sexually intimidated and sometimes raped in their hostels, leading to unwanted pregnancies and dropping out of school.

Not only do boy students rape the girls, school teachers take advantage of their position and coerces their girl students to engage in sex. A school teacher was accused of luring a Standard Five pupil returning home from church. He took her to his house, claiming he wanted to send her on an errand, but locked her up and raped her.

HIV/AIDS

During the 1990s the Kenya newspapers were bursting with articles on the HIV epidemic and the prevalence of AIDS. The first case of HIV/AIDS in Kenya was found in 1984. The World Health Organization representative in Kenya said that AIDS originated in Kenya from tourists, though a common belief is that it originated in Central Africa.

By 1995 HIV/AIDS had become a national disaster with 200,000 known dead and 10% of the population infected with the HIV virus. The "medical holocaust" was killing 111 Kenyans daily in 1996. UNICEF reported that Kenya was among the top three countries in Africa with the highest incidence of AIDS. By comparison the United States of America had 441,528 cases of HIV/AIDS in 1995, compared to 418,051 for the whole continent of Africa.

The highest rate of infections among ethnic communities was found in western Kenya, especially among the Luo, ranging from 20% in Kisumu to 25% in Homa Bay. The homosexuals (lesbian, gay, bisexual, transgender, and queer – the LGBTQ+ community – they are still adding) were the first to be hit. The so-called sex workers had the highest rate of infection at 30%, and the young, ages 20-35, had the highest number of individuals infected.

HIV/AIDS is contracted through sexual encounters with infected partners. Sex workers are the most obvious, but when anyone becomes infected, perhaps unknowingly, he or she passes on the HIV infection with the next sex partner. The most tragic situation arises when an unfaithful husband contracts HIV through adultery and then infects his pure, innocent wife. The most heinous crime occurs when an infected mother transmits the HIV virus to her unborn child through the placenta. Tens of thousands of children in Kenya are born with HIV/AIDS.

HIV/AIDS can also be transmitted through intravenous needles shared with drug-users, or through contaminated blood transmissions. Out of fear of contracting HIV/AIDS, many Kenyans refused transmission of other people's blood and instead banked their own blood. It is clear that not everyone with AIDS has contracted it from unfaithful sexual activity.

Efforts to Combat Moral Decline and HIV/AIDS

The primary way in which the government sought to alleviate the spread of HIV/AIDS was by promoting "safe sex" through the use of condoms, and the introduction of "sex education" in schools.

Their secular wisdom was simple. Studies had shown that 4% of adolescents engage in sex before the age of ten, a slim majority do so by the age of 14 and a vast majority by the age of 16. As one gynecologist observed, sexual activity among the youth is a reality despite all the preaching in churches, and it is only logical that "safe sex" be taught.

The blame for this is the breakdown of traditional African culture. In the past, grandmothers taught the children about sex. Since this cultural tradition has become obsolete for many, youth tend to learn it from one another and through experimentation.

Through the help of overseas benefactors, condoms have become readily available in Kenya. Advocates of condoms asserted that the surest way of preventing HIV/AIDS and sexually transmitted disease was through condoms, though they admitted, abstention from sex and faithfulness were the best.

However the promoters of condoms failed to tell the whole truth. While condoms *reduce* the infection rate, they are not 100% reliable. Studies have shown a 12% failure rate when used by adults and a 40% rate of failure when used by adolescents.

Promotion of condoms included the movie, *More Time,* which eulogized condoms and threw cold water on the idea of chastity until marriage and faithfulness in marriage. Nowhere did the movie warn that condoms cannot guarantee "safe sex," only less risk.

Anyone who desires to be certain that he or she will not end up with a sexually transmitted disease, including HIV/AIDS, should abstain from sex until marriage and remain faithful in marriage. But this was not the promotional pitch being made. The assumption was that the sex drive was uncontrollable and the only way to prevent AIDS was through condoms. The question of God and his holy law were never stated, only "safe sex."

The really big controversy centered on the government's plan of introducing sex education in schools. The government's concern was not only to find ways of reducing the spread of HIV/AIDS, but reducing Kenya's population explosion. As a pilot project the "sex" education had been taught in 56 schools since 1987, but in 1994 the government wanted to introduce it nationwide. News reports, articles, editorials and letters to the editor flooded the paper during the years of 1994-1995.

Sex education is allegedly too hot a subject to be handled in Africa so the government's plan was to introduce into the school curriculum of Standards Five to Eight a subject called "Family Life Education" which encompassed sex, population and social education. The idea was to educate the youth about becoming adults, learning of sexual issues and family planning.

Churches and parents raised a united voice against this proposal. They feared that the teaching of "sex" in schools would encourage promiscuity.

Though the curriculum was called "Family Life Education," in reality it was "sex" education. The Roman Catholic Church planned mass action countrywide against "sex" lessons taught in school. They were specifically concerned about the promotion of condoms, contraceptives and abortions.

The pushback paid off initially when the State decided to rethink "sex" education. However, the government secretly continued their plans and eventually introduced the "Family Life Education" into the Kenyan schools. Their concern was the large number of girls who had to drop out of school because of pregnancies. They desired to teach the consequences associated with sexual activity.

However, the churches contended that "sex" education was the responsibility of the family and the church which had moral concerns. Adolescents need more than knowledge of sex and how to avoid the consequences of engaging in sex. They need the moral dimension that is missing in government schools.

APATHY

Apathy is lack of compassion, lack of love, and lack of concern for others. Apathetic people are disinterested in the needs around them. They remain passive in the face of want. In brief, apathy is the absence of love for others. Loving your neighbor as yourself is absent with apathy.

Institutions

Many of society's social ills are due to apathy. Take for example the institutions run by the government. How much better care would be given to patients in hospitals if the doctors, nurses, interns, assistants and caretakers felt compassion and concern for their patients?

Government Hospitals: Patients with experience in many government hospitals can better explain the pain and suffering caused by calloused hearts – long waiting times, neglect, absence of care and concern, indifference to the suffering, lack of medical supplies and bedding, and just plain apathy toward the sick and needy.

Reported problems in the hospitals were numerous: because a hospital had run out of a particular drug, a patient who was bitten by a scorpion was told to buy the drug elsewhere and seek the help from another nurse; bodies of the dead were left in the hospital wards for long periods; the decomposing body of a middle-aged man was left in the ward for five days before being removed to the mortuary; in another case the relatives of the deceased were told that no one was willing to be in contact with the dead man until the relatives purchased gloves for the mortuary attendants. Consequently, the decaying body remained in the hospital ward for days.

One MP, who toured a District Hospital, was appalled. "What we have witnessed," he declared," is a frightening spectacle of neglect and abandonment that defy human imagination." In other words, *apathy* – lack of compassionate love – was the underlying problem.

Prisons: The Kenya Human Rights Commission inspected government prisons and declared that Kenya's prisons were some of the most "cruel, inhuman and horrifying in the world." Instead of being rehabilitating centers, they had become "dungeons of death." Pushed by hunger, prisoners ate their own waste. Lack of water caused prisoners to wash with their own urine. Prison overcrowding was a massive problem. Kenya's prisons in the 1990s were eight fewer than at independence in 1963, yet the prison population has grown threefold.

Torture and inhumane treatment was often meted out, even though this is forbidden by the Constitution and the Prison Act. Young convicts were forced into homosexuality, causing several to be admitted into the hospital because they were so badly sodomized. The result was a higher percentage of HIV/AIDS cases among prisoners than in free society.

Roads

The roads in Kenya during the 1980s and 1990s were potholed and treacherous. Driving in Kenya can also be hazardous because of reckless drivers on deteriorating roads.

Bold headlines tell of the dangers: "12 perish as bus goes up in flames;" "19 killed in two road accidents;" "Road accidents 'alarming' – 329,000 killed, hurt since independence" [1962-1995]; "7 die in 35 daily accidents in Kenya;" "17,000 died on the road last year" (1986). A family of six perished as they returned home from a wedding when their pick-up collided with a petrol tanker. The death toll per vehicle on Kenyan roads is 40 times higher than in the United States and Europe.

Kenyan drivers are risk takers, overtaking vehicles recklessly around the curves and below the crest of a hill when the way forward is not visible. It is amazing what "civilization" can do to African drivers. They have moved from a relaxed, event oriented society to a rushed, clock oriented society, greedy for money. Every minute for the *matatu* driver is *pesa*, so they risk it all for money. They speed and violate every standard of courtesy. The result is not minor bumper accidents, but head-on collisions which totally and completely demolish the vehicles. Speed and poor judgment kill.

Taking a bus from Eldoret to Nairobi forced me to pray more earnestly than on most other occasions. Two bus drivers decided to race each other, recklessly and carelessly passing each other around curves and in face of oncoming traffic. It was a terrifying experience for me. My prayers were answered when the other bus took a different route and our bus driver settled down, driving more sanely down the escarpment to Nakuru.

During the 1980s and 1990s the road conditions were deplorable with crater-like potholes, and stretches where the tarmac had disappeared. Shock absorbers, tires, rims, suspension, and steering system alignments were damaged from poor roads.

During the 1990s the Nairobi/Mombasa road became impassable during the rains. In 1998 the Mombasa road was closed because of the collapse of a bridge. Hundreds of truck drivers were stranded for four days. Through the help of the army a temporary bridge was constructed which allowed lighter vehicles to cross.

Investors became worried over the condition of the roads, reporting that millions of shillings were being lost daily due to the deplorable condition of the roads. Bold headlines declared that the Mombasa road was a "bane on our national pride." The government promised to enlist foreign assistance to remedy the road situation and by the time of this publication the Nairobi/Mombasa road had been rebuilt.

Urban Blight

Much has been written about the tragic condition of cities like Nairobi and Mombasa. Within the city of Nairobi are approximately 200 unregulated settlements with 2,600,000 slum dwellers, 60% of Nairobi's population residing on 6% of the land. The largest in Kenya is Kibera, the largest slum in all of Africa with 250,000 people.

These slum areas were plagued with mountains of rotting, vermin infested garbage, uncollected for weeks. In Mombasa during seasons of monsoon rains, the poor sanitation spreads bodily waste throughout the slums, led to scores of deaths from water borne diseases with reports of 4,000 cases of cholera and diarrhea.

Homa Bay, lying along Lake Victoria, suffered from tons of fish by-products dumped in the town. The flies attracted to this smelly, rotting filth became so numerous that workers in nearby offices had to vacate their office buildings temporarily because of the pesky invasion of flies.

Big cities are troubled with parking boys and street children, desperately trying to hold on to life – begging, bag-snatching and stealing whatever they can find. Street mothers, many sexually abused and fleeing from their paternal homes, reside on the streets with their children, begging for food. Hawkers set up their stands on city sidewalks and pester pedestrians, trying to sell their wares.

Cities are unsafe. Traffic lights don't work. Without street lights, darkness breeds all kinds of evil. The "Machakos 'airport'" in Nairobi is treacherous at dusk. After dark thieves snatch luggage, purses, watches, and in some cases, they tear off women's blouses, searching their busts in the hopes of finding money safely tucked away.

Due to lack of city planning and the inundation of privately owned vehicles, the city streets of Nairobi are a nightmare: traffic jams are caused by the glut of car imports, traffic lights seldom working, and daredevil drivers pushing and shoving without any courtesy for others. The roads are chockablock full with cars driving on the pavement.

In addition, massive potholes impede the traffic, and rain flooded thoroughfares become impassable. On certain roads the potholes extended across the whole width of the road, causing nightmares for drivers, especially during the rainy season.

CONCLUSION

The social ills described in this chapter were not derived from hearsay. They were all taken directly from Kenyan newspaper reports which were written by courageous and transparent Kenyan journalists.

Though newspapers from other African nations have not been read, from my personal visits to numerous other African nations, and talking with my students and graduates from other African countries, I believe these social ills described in this chapter are found throughout the African continent.

What is also abundantly clear is that these social problems in Africa are not unique to Africa. Western nations, Middle Eastern nations and Asian nations have the same problems. Africa may have uniquely African manifestations of human depravity, but they are not alone because all human beings are sons and daughters of Adam and Eve who fell into sin and passed their fallen human nature onto their offspring.

2

THE FAMILY AND STATE

God has ordained two social institutions to hold society together: the **Family** to nurture their children so that they will grow into godly, responsible young men and women, and the **State** to protect society from the inevitable evils that come from sinful offspring. These are the two building blocks of any human society mandated at Creation.

THE FAMILY

In the creation account of Genesis we read that it was *not good* for the first man to be alone. He needed a companion. From the side of Adam God created the first woman and brought her to Adam.

"'At last,' Adam exclaimed, 'She is part of my own flesh and bone! She will be called 'woman,' because she was taken out of a man. This explains why a man leaves his father and mother and is joined to his wife, and the two are united into one" (Ge 2:23-24).

To this first married couple God issued three mandates: (1) Obey my commandments; (2) Multiply and fill the earth, and (3) Subdue the earth (Ge 1:28).

Obey my Commandments

When God created Adam he planted a beautiful garden and placed the first man in it. *"But the Lord God gave him this warning: 'You may freely eat any fruit in the garden except fruit from the tree of knowledge of good and evil. If you eat of its fruit, you will surely die"* (Ge 2:16-17). Even before Adam and Eve had children, they disobeyed the first mandate.

After Eve was brought to Adam to be his companion and helper, Satan appeared in the form of a serpent and tempted the woman to doubt God's Word and to disobey him.

"The woman was convinced. The fruit looked so fresh and delicious, and it would make her wise. So she ate some of the fruit. She also gave some to her husband, who was with her. Then he ate it too" (Ge 3:6).

Adam had failed in leadership of his home. God had given to the husband the responsibility of headship in the home. But Adam failed.

After this grievous sin, the whole human race became sinful in their natures. The first-born son became jealous of his younger brother. He erupted in anger and killed him (Ge 4:1-12). *"The human heart is most deceitful and desperately wicked. Who really knows how bad it is?* (Jer 17:9). Hatred and violence began filling the earth. In fact the wickedness of humanity grew so great that *"all their thoughts were consistently and totally evil"* (Ge 6:5). So God sent the worldwide flood to destroy the rebellious human race, saving only Noah and his family. Every society on earth among all races and languages has reflected this sinful nature.

Multiply and Fill the Earth with Godly Children

The one mandate that the human race has kept with abandonment is to multiply and fill the earth with their children. By 2019 the population grew to 7,700,000,000 human beings. But the nature of human beings has remained the same, *"deceitful and desperately wicked."*

And most fathers, like Adam, have failed to give faithful leadership in the home by serving the Lord. God's intention was that through godly teaching and example, each child would be nurtured to fear God and obey his commandments. But parents have failed miserably.

So God chose Abraham and his descendants and made a covenant with Israel. God promised to be their God and they would be his people. He gave them covenant obligations found in the Ten Commandments. Repeatedly God instructed the adult Hebrews to obey the commandments which he had given, and also to teach them to their children.

"Teach them to your children. Talk about them when you are at home and when you are away on a journey, when you are lying down and when you are getting up again. Write them on the doorposts of your house and on your gates, so that as long as the sky remains above the earth, you and your children may flourish in the land the LORD swore to give your ancestors" (Dt 11:19-21).

The commandments mandating morality were few in number:

1. Do not worship any other gods besides me.
2. Do not make idols of any kind.
3. Do not misuse the name of the LORD your God.
4. Remember the Sabbath day by keeping it holy.
5. Honor your father and mother.
6. Do not murder.

7. Do not commit adultery.
8. Do not steal.
9. Do not testify falsely against your neighbor.
10. Do not covet.

In addition to the Ten Commandments, there were ceremonial and civil commandments pertaining to their worship and civil society, a total of 613 commandments.

The two greatest commandments are these: First and foremost, "*You must love the Lord your God with all your heart, and all your soul, and all your mind*" (Dt 6:5). The second greatest commandment is equally important: "*Love your neighbor as yourself*" (Lev 19:18; See Mt 22:37-39). All Ten Commandments are fulfilled when obeying these two (Gal 5:14).

It is the parents who are responsible to instruct and teach their children to obey God's commandments. Mothers have a vital role since they are with their children much of the day. But Scripture assigns the primary responsibility for spiritual leadership in the home specifically to the fathers: "*And now a word to you fathers. Don't make your children angry by the way you treat them. Rather, bring them up with the discipline and instruction approved by the Lord*" (Eph 6:4). Only when families are fulfilling their responsibilities will society become wholesome and good.

According to God's instruction in the New Testament, a healthy, clean-living, honest family is where husbands love their wives as they love their own bodies, and where wives submit to the loving leadership of the husband as the Church submits to Christ, and where children learn to obey their parents (Eph 5:21-6:3). Only when this takes place will societies become what God intended.

Many early converts to the Christian faith in Kenya were faithful, not only taking their children to church, but leading their families in daily family worship. This led to church growth as their children grew up strong in the Christian faith, living a life worthy of the Gospel and becoming lights in society.

Whenever parents, led by the father, faithfully teach their children daily the Word of God and lead them in prayer during family worship, the results are undeniable. One Kalenjin family with six boys and five girls is a sterling example. The parents exhorted their children to trust in God.

Every morning and evening the family had compulsory devotions with singing, praying and reading of Scripture. Even when parents were not present, the older siblings led in the family worship. Every evening a time was given for each person to read quietly a passage of Scripture of his or her own choice. After some time each child would explain to the family what he or she had read and what it meant to them. In addition, the father took time to talk with each of his children personally about the Gospel and their need of a Savior. He also encouraged each child to enter full-time Christian ministry. By God's grace all eleven children are serving the Lord in one capacity or another as Christian leaders.

If for some reason the father does not assume his rightful role as the spiritual head of the home, God has entrusted the mother with the responsibility to teach her children God's Word, to pray with and for them and to lead them into a personal faith in Jesus Christ.

Subdue the Earth for Improvement in Life

These well taught, respectable and responsible families are then mandated to "*subdue*" the earth (Ge 1:28). This is what God commanded Adam and Eve.

A further statement clarifies God's intention. After God planted a garden and placed Adam in it, he directed Adam to "*tend and care for it*" (Ge 2:15). (The English Standard Version translates this in this way: "*work it and take care of it.*") The command to *subdue* the earth and *tend and care for it* has been called the Creation Mandate. This is the work that God gave to Adam and Eve and all their descendants at creation before their sinful rebellion. It is a continuing mandate to this day.

The English word, *to work* the garden, means "*to till the earth and cultivate it.*" In other words, Adam and Eve were commanded to be good farmers. The English word, "culture," comes from the Latin word "*cultura*" which in Middle English (A.D. 1,150-1,500) meant "*cultivation of the soil,*" that is, preparing the soil for planting of crops. One thousand years ago the English word, *culture*, referred to the cultivation of the soil in farming. Over time new meaning attached to the English word "*culture,*" so that "culture" now refers to a way of life, the improvement and refinement of the way of life by training and study.

Taken in this broader meaning of "culture," the Creation Mandate means that families of the human race should both cultivate the soil to provide food to eat, and study and learn through experimentation how they might develop and improve their lifestyle by "subduing" the resources which God has provided in the earth.

This means that human beings, grouped in families, were mandated to improve their way of life with horticultural methods and implements as they farmed the land (Ge 2:15). We find in the early chapters of Genesis that human beings did develop culture and improve their lives. They developed engineering skills and discovered different building supplies to construct dwellings and build cities (Ge 4:17). Soon after creation animal husbandry improved with the domestication of animals for personal use (Ge 4:20). Even musical skills were developed as they crafted musical instruments for their enjoyment (Ge 4:20). Metallurgy began early as they mined and utilized earth's metals (Ge 4:22).

Even though Adam and Eve and their descendants (the human race) were mandated to *till the earth and cultivate it* in order to improve their lifestyle, they were to do this as vice-regents of God in service to God. Adam and Eve were commanded to rule the earth on God's behalf for his glory. The earth is God's creation. He is the sovereign Lord. As Scripture says: "*The earth is the LORD's, and everything in it. The world and all its people belong to him. For he laid the earth's foundation on the seas and built it on the ocean depths*" (Ps 24:1f).

The Garden of Eden was God's creation, and human beings as vice-regents of God were required to do their work responsibly. Environmental degradation is the result of human greed and avarice, caring more for selfish gain than being good stewards of creation as God made it. Sinful men and women have despoiled the earth and its beauty by polluting it.

Contemporary Family Life

The danger of stereotyping society is that it tends to pre-judge everyone and it overlooks the good. Newspapers notoriously report <u>bad news</u>, it seldom reports good news. The wonderful fact is that many wonderful, faithful Christian families thrive in Kenya despite the social ills surrounding them.

Nevertheless, newspapers do report genuine problems in society. So what do we read of families in Kenya? Are they all living counter cultural lives, faithfully loving and obeying God's Word, or are they reflecting the social ills of society?

Drunkenness: Husbands sometimes waste their money and destroy their marriages by drinking. Bars and night clubs attract men who drink in excess into the night. When they return home in a drunken state chaos erupts. All kinds of abuse arises from inebriated men.

Battered Wives: Violent husbands, often drunk, abuse their wives with slaps and fists. Worse yet, repeated and severe beatings lead to battered wives. It is a known fact that for every one battered woman who seeks help or takes refuge elsewhere, there are many others who conceal their injuries and hide their marital problems. Despite the noble efforts in Kenya to curb the disturbing practice of beating and raping women, violence against women continues to rise. In an effort to counter crimes against women, gender-related NGOs planned campaigns against gender violence.

Child Abuse: Wasting money on alcohol and adultery results in child neglect and abuse. They are beaten by the father, forced into child labor, neglected, and driven to forge for food in dumps. In one reported case the father defiled his eleven year old daughter. Other times mothers abandoned their children. In another case a new born infant was thrown into a pit latrine by the mother with the father nowhere to be found.

In one such dysfunctional home an eleven year-old son of a policeman gabbed his father's gun and shot his own father. An editorial on child abuse headlined: "The cases are endless." One editorial asked the question, "Is child abuse in Kenya a reflection of a 'collective moral bankruptcy'?"

Family Violence: The following headlines tell the tragic tale of family violence: "MP stabs wife in family fight," "Man kills his mother," "Father brutally killed two of his children," "Woman tortures her teenage daughter to death and secretly buries her," "Mother poisons her 4 children," "Woman plotted murder of husband," "Man gets 7 years for killing wife over sex," "Man burnt his pregnant wife and confined her to the house for 41 days," "Man kills daughter for spilling 'chang'aa,'" "Man beheads his brother," "Man slashes wife to death," "Mother kills her three-year old daughter," and "Mother sets son's arms ablaze."

Breakdown of Traditional African Values: Because of urbanization, western forms of education, introduction of modern technology and the westernization of Africa, African traditions are breaking down. For many Africans nothing substantial has replaced traditional family values. For many the Christian faith has not taken deep roots. With the breakdown of families, African society is suffering.

Traditionally, children were taught to respect their elders, indeed, required to revere them. They learned the discipline of obedience, respect, and work. Parental control was exercised during the courtship days. Africans loved and prized children. The extended family cared for the elderly.

In these days parental instruction is often lacking, especially teaching by the father. Parents fail to instill discipline in their children. Obedience is either not required or harsh discipline is meted out which only exasperates the youth. Children can no longer wander safely by themselves in the towns and cities. With the loss of communal chaperoning, youth engage in alcohol, drugs, casual sex with condoms or without. Instead of parents instilling traditional or Christian values in the children and youth, they imbibe a licentious worldview by watching movies, TV and videos. Westernization has had an insidious effect on African youth who are not reared in Christian homes with faithful living and nurturing.

Parental advice is ignored when marriage is considered. Youth marry in haste and regret afterwards. A surprising number of young adults, both male and female, prefer the single life and pleasure without the responsibility of caring for children. The aged no longer face a secure future, but one fraught with loneliness and want.

Thoughtless adaption of western values, which today are pagan and non-Christian, is causing the peoples to jump mindlessly out of the frying pan and into the fire.

Conclusion

Hopefully, these newspaper reports of the breakdown of family values with family violence are the exception. Many strong Christian homes can be found in the cities and rural areas. But these reports do reflect deep problems of drunkenness, drug abuse, land disputes and extra-marital sexual relationships. At the core of these problems is the lack of genuine love, faithfulness and self-control – a lack of Christian character.

The tragedy is that Kenya is not unique in their family problems. The United States suffers from the same basic underlying causes with the family unit disintegrating. In many respects, America is worse off because civil society no longer respects, admires or adheres to Christian precepts.

Over 40% of all children born in the United States are born out of wedlock (70% for African-Americans). Nearly 70% of all American children do not grow up with both their biological parents. The makeup of homes has changed significantly since the sexual revolution of the 1960s with two-parent homes rearing children dropping from 88% to 69% today. Single mothers with children number 23%. Fifteen million Americans live together as unmarried couples, a whopping 138% increase since 1960. Marriage of gay couples is now legal.

Divorce in America is common and easy to obtain with 50% of all marriages ending in the divorce courts. All States recognize "No Fault Divorces." This means that it takes only a few weeks to be divorced. The average length of marriages is eight years.

One in four women and one in seven men have been physically abused in their intimate relationships, ranging from slapping, shoving and pushing to severe physical violence like beating, burning, strangling and killing.

When the basic building block of society (the family) is not living in accordance with God's Word – husbands loving their wives as they love themselves, wives submitting to their husbands as the church submits to Christ, and children obeying their parents – the whole fabric of society begins to tear apart.

GOVERNING AUTHORITY

Human beings are social creatures, created by God to live in a structured society under God's rule. God is the one who instituted authorities to govern people. These "governing authorities" are necessary in this fallen, sinful world because of the need to restrain evil.

No one form of government is preferred in Scripture. Throughout history governing authorities have included *chiefdoms* (ruled by chiefs), *monarchies* (ruled by emperors and kings), *oligarchies* (ruled by a small elite), *dictatorships* (ruled by despots), *democracies* (direct rule of the people), *and republics* (ruled by the elected representatives of the people). No government is better than the leaders who govern.

Biblical Teaching

Because of the human condition with everyone's heart being "desperately wicked," every form of human government has failed. But experience has shown that "power corrupts and absolute power corrupts absolutely." Therefore, the best form of government is limited government with either a democracy with direct rule by the people or a republic whose leaders are chosen by the people. But even democracies fail because of corruption and greed. The constitution and laws are only as good as their enforcement.

Above all earthly rule is the LORD God who is King of kings, and Lord of lords. He rules in his eternal kingdom over his creation, directing human history towards its consummation when Jesus Christ himself will be the beneficent Lord governing the people with justice (Da 4:34-35; 6:26-27). In the meantime God has instituted governing authorities. *"All governments have been placed in power by God"* (Ro 13:1b).

Every society is filled with individuals who abuse and plunder people through corrupt leadership with theft, violence, lust and the absence of any compassion. Governing authorities have been ordained by God to help people by protecting them and by punishing all evil doers. *"The authorities are sent by God to help you…The authorities are established by God for that very purpose to punish those who do wrong"* (Ro 13:4).

Christians are commanded to pray for governing authorities (1 Ti 2:1f), and to obey them (Ro 13:1, 5). This includes respecting and honoring them, paying taxes and doing only what is lawful (Ro 13:6-7). Paul gave this command to obey and respect governing authorities when Israel was under the colonial rule of Rome which was ruthless and cruel. Obedience and respect can be painful under these circumstances, but it is biblical.

However, whenever governing authorities order their subjects to do anything that is contrary to the will of the sovereign Lord, Christians must obey God rather than their government leaders (Ac 4:19-20; 5:29).

Christians may protest and passively resist unjust governments when done without violence. Calling governments to uphold just and humane governance is biblical when done with love and humility. Any Christian engaged in non-violent protest should be willing to accept meekly their arrest and punishment by the governing authorities.

Contemporary Experience

Thank God for government efforts to protect innocent citizens and punish those who terrorize society. The tragedy is that the social ills of society are found in government as well.

Violence: Police brutality is a problem. They beat suspects in order to extract confessions or information, leading to serious injuries and worse, even painful deaths. Suspects die in custody, or in the hospital where they are treated for their life-threatening wounds. As one headline noted: "Elite unit – turned terror squad. They left a trail of blood and tears." Police kill suspected gangsters, street boys, and students during protest rallies. The result is that many Kenyans fear the police and would rather not have anything to do with them.

Corruption: Dishonesty by government officials is endemic in Kenya. Greedy citizens run for political office in order to become wealthy.

The country has reportedly lost billions of shillings through corrupt dealings of government officials. In 1995 Kenya was warned that high-level, widespread corruption threatened her economic and political future.

There are many different ways for those in power to gain dishonest profit by using their position and authority.

The Shimoni area on Kenya's South Coast was made a marine reserve to preserve the national treasures of multi-colored tropical fish and exquisite coral reef formations. But Chale Island within the marine reserve was given to a politician who then sold it to a foreign developer who has developed it into a prime tourist destination, thwarting noble environmental goals.

Calls were made to the government to stop the land-grabbing mania and retrieve the land for their rightful owners, but the results were mixed.

A form of political corruption is graft in which individuals use bribery to gain influence from authorities to circumvent the law for personal gain.

Senior government officials in positions of power and privilege sold houses that did not belong to them. They stole property from the State by selling what did not belong to them.

Policemen extorted money from a secondhand clothes dealer after inspection of his goods, and threatened his arrest if he were not paid.

Politicians handed out money to win elections. An MP gave out food to clash victims in order to induce them to vote for him. Accompanying him was a Roman Catholic priest who told the crowd that if they voted for KANU they would be voting for "killers, arsonists, and cattle rustlers."

Such corruption can be found at all levels of government. On one occasion two policemen took a bribe from the driver of an overloaded *matatu*. One of the passengers was the CID director who charged them for the offense. Following this the editor of the newspaper commended the CID director, but observed that these policemen were the little fish. They knew full well that their bosses were also corrupt and would overlook their wrongdoing because they also took bribes, yet they continued on with their corruption.

Using trickery and deceit to gain unfair advantage for personal gain is fraudulent. Oxfam accused the Kenyan government officials of treating their countries' wealth as personal funds. There are many ways of wrongfully deceiving during financial transactions including swindling (cheating) and embezzling (misappropriation of funds).

Customs Officers presented false customs import entry forms for clearing the container of radio cassettes, thus denying the government of the customs and excise duty and VAT for the imported cassettes.

The Nairobi City Hall siphoned millions of shillings from the government by employing "ghost workers." Citizens, through their payment of taxes, enriched City Hall officials through this scheme.

City of Nairobi allocated plots to government officials who then sold them back to National Social Security Fund at exorbitant prices, double and triple the estimated value. The NSSF bought flats for a stated price, but received only half that amount.

Forgery of documents is a common method of fraud. Ministers of Parliament were jailed for altering documents. Printers cheated by forging paper currency, such as Sh500 notes. VAT inspectors collude with companies to forge receipts and assessment forms that deny the Treasury millions of shillings in revenue.

The Goldenberg scandal outraged the international community. Countless numbers of judges and ministers of government were implicated in this scam which cost the Kenyan government an estimated 10% of its annual Gross Domestic Product.

In a government approved scheme, Goldenberg International was compensated for Kenyan gold sold in order to bring in much needed foreign currency. But the government subsidized Goldenberg 35% more than the alleged foreign currency received. Further, the gold available for export from Kenya's one gold mine could not account for the large amounts allegedly sold. Either not much gold was actually sold or gold was smuggled into Kenya illegally from the Congo. The government officers received kickbacks for their participation, a rip-off deal that tax payers needed to pay.

Lust: Two girls were walking to an evening church service when two armed policemen caught them and raped them behind a toilet. When they screamed people came to their rescue, but the policemen pointed their guns at them and everyone fled.

The newspaper reports go on and on and on with these tragic accounts. One girl, walking to her high school, was abducted, confined for three months and raped repeatedly every day, up to ten times daily. A mother was waylaid by three men, dragged into a coffee plantation and raped for hours.

Newspapers in America seldom publish such problems. But it is reported that every 92 seconds, an American is sexually assaulted. Every nine minutes that victim is a child. One out of every six American women has been the victim of an attempted or actual rape in her lifetime. Lust of the flesh is a universal scourge.

Stealing Famine Food: Parts of Kenya are prone to drought. Every few years the rains fail. The result is famine and starvation. The hungry scavenge for anything edible. In these cases the government provides famine relief, but apathy toward the hungry can be a scandalous problem.

Accusations were made that the government was politicizing the relief food distribution, starving the opposition strongholds. Nine MPs from Nyanza Province appealed for relief food, claiming that their people had been bypassed. Worse than this, chiefs, their assistants and government officials seized the famine food and sold it for personal gain. Greedy, well-to-do leaders think of themselves first, leaving pittance for the starving.

During the dreadful famine of 1997 the Kamba in Kitui South watched helplessly as their loved ones died of starvation. One man in Ikutha hung himself to avoid the agony of dying without food. During this very same famine leaders cashed in on famine relief and grabbed land for personal gain.

Injustice: Injustice is lack of fairness. Partiality due to prejudice and undue pressure becomes a miscarriage of justice. Bribery and favoritism contribute to injustice. At its heart, injustice is indifference to the basic rights of others. Love of neighbor should lead to fairness. Apathy is disinterest in the wellbeing of others and this leads to injustice.

Injustice wreaks havoc on society and causes all kinds of social ills. The poor without land nail together a shelter with throwaway iron sheets and timber on an empty plot. In this lodging the mother and her six children accumulated their paltry possessions to support their measly lifestyle: dishes, blankets, clothes, school uniforms, and a tiny stash of cash.

Suddenly on a Sunday morning, a bulldozer crashed through this slum settlement, demolishing everything in the name of Kenya Railways Corporation which claimed their land. The hapless residents were unable to salvage any of their possessions because the guards beat anyone who tried. Without a roof over their heads and despoiled of all their possessions, the poor became poorer still. Who will defend the poor?

Criminologists and legal experts lamented that the Kenya judicial system favors the rich. Double standards treat the rich more leniently, and the poor more harshly. The rich hire great lawyers while the poor are convicted.

Street children, abandoned by their parents, turn to street life for survival. Filled with confusion, insecurity, fear and even depression, they grapple for means to survive: begging, lying and stealing. Death eventually takes their lives from disease, drug abuse, malnutrition, accidents and mob justice. Police, trying to maintain law and order, and to protect the innocent passersby, harshly beat them, maiming them and causing mortal harm. Where is the compassion and justice to deal with societal ills?

Most critics blame the problem on poverty, but poverty in most cases is only a symptom, not the primary cause. Many families are dysfunctional, lacking the wisdom, love and maturity to care for their children. They are unaware of the need to space their children and limit their number so that they can provide adequate support. Money is squandered with alcohol, drugs and other vices. Fathers are unfaithful to their wives and unsupportive of their children. "It is the children's parents who should be arrested, not the children," declared one newspaper.

Experience has shown that with love and care these street children can thrive in school and do well in society. Justice is not meted out when society does not help the struggling poor with compassionate love and care.

"Mob justice" is by definition injustice because the accused has no opportunity of self-defense in the court of justice. On the other hand, "mob justice" is common because the masses of people do not believe in the integrity of the justice system. Police are bribed who then release the guilty. As a result, the mob takes justice in their own hands and mete out punishment by themselves, sometimes brutal and even fatal.

Injustice of course is a human condition which plagues every nation. For Kenyans injustice began when the British colonized the East African Protectorate, now known as Kenya. Under the British legal system the indigenous peoples of the land were deprived of their land rights in favor of the invaders. Injustice continues to this day in the independent Kenya.

A common complaint in the United States is that, despite its claim to be a nation of laws, the rich and powerfully connected often escape the just penalty of their crimes, while the poor pay for their crimes in full.

Political Fights: Not only do politicians duel with each other with words, they also fight with their fists. Pandemonium broke out in Parliament when "legislators punched each other, grabbed at the mace and shouted…" Death threats were uttered and a wife feared for her legislator husband's life.

Newspaper headliners tell it all: "Political parties erupt with internal feuds," a "Generation war erupts in Meru," "Kenyans need a movement, not warring parties," "Echoes of the past in succession 'war,'" "Chaos forces poll extension," "Fracas erupts at Kajiado polls" and "Polls official 'caught erasing ballot papers.'"

Conclusion

When the State fails to fulfill God's mandate of protecting her citizens from those who would harm them, great suffering occurs. In certain nations horrific anguish has taken place. Throughout the communist rule of Russia, 100 million people died at the hand of the State. During the four years of the Great Leap Forward under China's Mao Zedong, 45 million were slaughtered, making this champion of socialist ideals the greatest mass murderer in world history.

Other national leaders are more benign. Through inept or corrupt leadership the nation falls into a state of anarchy where private citizens protect themselves from lawless men. Some nations are led by egotistical, self-centered "Big Men" who swindle the nation's wealth. Others, through incompetent leadership, lead their country into economic ruin. Leaders in America are more constrained by law and the people, but subtly enrich themselves through corruption.

National corruption is endemic worldwide, though some nations are more corrupt than others. What is needed is God-fearing men and women who seek to obey "the royal law" which says: "*Love your neighbor as yourself*" (Ja 2:8); and as Jesus taught: "*Do for others as you would like them to do for you*" (Lk 6:31).

Not until we have leaders who follow these Christian truths, will we have national governments who adhere to justice, honesty and good governance.

3

THE CHRISTIAN CHURCH

The social ills in human societies should be no surprise. The sins of egotism, greed, lust and apathy have been part of the human story among all peoples from the beginning. The State, entrusted by God to protect its citizens and punish the wrongdoers, has failed to fulfill her God-given responsibility. No surprise! Can anyone find a government anywhere in the world which is just and fair and without corrupting greed?

And the family? If the family is the basic building block of every society, the tragedy is that the State is a reflection of a majority of families – a failure of the parents, especially the father, to nurture their children in the way they should go.

But what of the Christian Church? How is the Church measuring up to God's holy standard? Aren't the leaders and members of the Christian Church supposed to be lights that sparkle brightly in the darkness of a godless society? Isn't the Church supposed to be salt which preserves society from too much rottenness (Mt 5:13-16)?

The "Christian presence" in Kenya is astonishing according to the Kenyan statistics. According to the Joshua Project in 2019, 78% of Kenya's 52,470,000 citizens are professing Christians. That includes 47.57% who are adherents of evangelical churches. We may rightfully assume, therefore, that a large majority of members of Parliament and government leaders at the regional and district levels are professing Christians.

Don't large numbers in Kenya profess to be Christian? Do they actually join in political wrangling and dishonesty? Can it be that these professing Christians in government are complicit in the corruption within Kenya?

The tragic truth is that many Christian churches themselves reflect the social ills of society. Instead of changing society for the better, these churches reflect society because they have accommodated to the culture.

NEWSPAPER REPORTS OF CHURCH FAILURES

Here is what we found reported in the newspapers.

Church Fights: The newspapers were filled with reports of church fights. Virtually every denomination was reported to have physical conflicts and fights, though we shall omit names. Read these headlines:

"Man dies in church fight," "Man, 50, killed in church fight," "Eight injured as church members fight in Karatina," "Christians fight in church," "Swords, hammers replace the Bible" in a peace loving Quaker church, "Police avert church clash," "Worshippers hurt in fight at church," "Man killed in church battle" while four others were critically injured when rival Christian factions fought during a sermon.

The headings go on and on: "Mutiny in the church," "More than 100 disillusioned former members are waging ferocious war against the Nairobi Christian Church...," "Officials lock out church faithful," and a parish council feared that more than 200 parishioners were planning to disrupt the service.

The lengthy factional struggle of leadership in one major Kenyan church denomination was widely publicized with front page headline news over many weeks. This included the suspension of one bishop, the resignation of another, and the ongoing election struggles of another.

"Prayer service held off road." This occurred when a court injunction forbade fifteen officials from entering the church. In another church, nine lay leaders defied excommunication and held a service beside the road. A church service ended when "the faithful" heckled and jeered the church leader. "Members locked out of church." "Elders eject priest from church" who then led his followers in worship outside the church building.

Letters to the editors plead: "Let us end fights in the church," and "Stop fighting in the church."

The cause of these church fights varies, but in most cases power struggles among leaders are the problem. Constitutions are changed to accommodate election wishes of an aspirant. Night meetings are held, exchange of money takes place, and backhanded deals occur. In many cases the factional warfare occurs quietly and without public reporting. In other cases the factions actually break out in physical conflict in the glare of newspaper reporting.

But seldom is the real cause of church fights and power struggles recognized. In one case the bishop explained that "the problems facing the diocese were social, cultural, ethnic, political, linguistic and economical." Nothing was mentioned of the spiritual problem which, according to Scripture, underlies every other explanation.

Immorality: The moral lapses of lay Christians are seldom covered by newspapers, though tragically, immorality does occur among lay Christians all too often. Neither are most of the moral failures of church leaders published, though they do become newsworthy when taken to court.

A bishop was taken to court and accused of 17 charges, including adultery. Frequent front page coverage followed the court case until the bishop resigned. Another pastor was stoned to death by an irate mob who accused him of a love affair with a married woman. "Pastor fined for threat to woman" was accused of threatening his landlady for refusing an affair with him. "Sex scam pastor removed" from his position after allegedly impregnating a school girl. "Pastor gets two years for rape."

Greed: Church leaders with their authority and access to church funds are frequently known to "misappropriate" money for personal gain. In plain English, they break the 8th commandment by stealing. The High Court was told that a bishop had received 50,000/Ksh as a bribe to restrain the enthronement of the Bishop-elect. A church was accused of grabbing a plot on which they erected their diocesan headquarters. Another church was accused of acquiring church land by fraud. Two priests were arrested over charges of extortion. A major headline read: "The Church in crisis – Leadership squabbles, graft and mismanagement have raised questions on the credibility of some sects and religious groups."

RELATIVE FAITHFULNESS OF CHURCHES

It would be totally unfair to paint all churches in Kenya as described by these newspapers. Churches and their leaders are in many ways better than the reports of the newspapers suggest. Nevertheless, the newspaper reports are not fictional accounts. They are tips of icebergs with more lying beneath the surface than what appears in public. In many respects the Kenyan churches are representative of churches throughout the past 2,000 years, some seeking to live up to God's standard of holiness and others falling short, some grievously short. America has had its share of high profile Christian leaders who have fallen in disgrace.

We read of seven different churches in the Book of Revelation (Rev 2-3), located in Asia Minor, known today as Turkey. They range from churches that were theologically strong but lacking in love, to churches that were poor materially but rich in faith; from churches that were lukewarm in their devotion to Christ, to those who were being persecuted for their vibrant faith; from orthodox churches to apostatizing churches. In other words, the seven churches represent all the different kinds of churches found throughout history, just as we find in Kenya.

Nevertheless, we are confronted with a conundrum. Why do we find so much corruption in Kenya if 78% of Kenyans claim to be Christian? Does the Christian faith condone corruption? Why don't professing Christians live up to the high standard of holiness demanded by God? The Bible teaches: *"as he who called you is holy, you also be holy in all your conduct, since it is written, 'You shall be holy, for I am holy'"* (1 Pe 1:15-16).

NEWSPAPER FAILURES TO REPORT GOOD NEWS

Thank God for the positive good that Christian churches bring to society. Without Christian churches, African societies would be vastly different. This can be said for most nations including the United Kingdom and the United States. Newspapers generally report bad news, not good news. We don't read the good news about churches in newspapers, but from history we know of the many good things that have come to all nations through the preaching of the Gospel of Jesus Christ.

Education: The British East African Protectorate was changed from an illiterate colony into a literate nation through the hundreds of Christian primary schools.

The purpose of these schools was to help all Christian converts become literate so that they could read the Bible. The practice of translating the Bible into the mother tongues of the peoples and providing an education so that Christians could read the Bible for themselves came out of the Protestant Reformation. This was revolutionary. William Tyndale was burned at the stake for the crime of translating the Bible into English from Greek and Hebrew. Christians cannot grow into maturity without careful instruction from the Word of God. This requires literacy. One can argue that Christian schooling gave birth to the struggle for independence.

Christian missions and now their daughter churches have built the vast array of primary and secondary schools which laid the educational foundation for Kenya and prepared her citizens for colleges and universities. Today Christian denominations operate universities.

Medical Facilities: Churches with their founding missions built and maintain some of the best hospitals in the nation. Their schools of nursing train hundreds of governmentally recognized nurses who staff hundreds of church related dispensaries around the nation.

Works of Charity: Through the churches' benevolence, they channel relief food to the drought stricken hungry, give hope to displaced farmers, and provide homes for the orphans.

Moral Teaching: Churches provide moral education. They uphold the sanctity of life and oppose the killing of unborn persons. They oppose State sanctioned abortions. Numerous churches play a significant role in dealing with the HIV/AIDS epidemic. They call for peace during times of strife. Their witness in prisons has turned criminals into law abiding citizens.

Translation of the Bible: The Bible Society of Kenya has overseen the translation, publication and distribution of the Bible throughout Kenya. In 1994 the Bible Society of Kenya celebrated 150 years since the translation of the *Kimvita Swahili Bible* and portions of the *Kikamba Bible* by Dr. J. Krapf which was done in 1844.

In order to translate the Bible into the vernacular it was necessary to create an alphabet, discover the grammar, and develop a dictionary of vocabulary. The very newspapers we have today are indebted to the Christian Church which reduced the African languages into a written text.

Pioneering of Radio: *Biblia Husema* pioneered Christian broadcasting in Kenya, providing the nation with Bible teaching and preaching, and with Christian music which both Presidents Kenyatta and Moi treasured.

Transformation of Lives: Most importantly, numerous churches preach the gospel of saving grace through Jesus Christ and call their attendees to repentance and faith in Christ. Through their conversion and discipleship thousands of Kenyans have lived honorable lives of integrity. Churches teach the Word of God to children, youth and adults in order to ground them in the principles of godly living.

The Bible and the Christian message taught in schools have made a lasting impact on Kenya's leadership after independence, including the first two presidents. Mzee Jomo Kenyatta read the Bible during his detention and thereafter favored Christian missions. His Excellency Daniel Arap Moi was profoundly shaped by the Christian message. At the dedication of the A.I.C. Milimani church site, President Moi declared that salvation comes from the Bible, not from abroad.

Failure of Christian Churches throughout History

What has been described in Kenya during the 20th century is similar to many churches in the West and throughout the past 2,000 years.

Take the example of the Christian Church in Europe in 1,300 A.D. During the Medieval age we find that the European Christian Church was frequently guilty of egotism, with shady tactics in power struggles, immorality, greed, and fraud. Here is one example a church leader.

Benedict Gaetani was born in 1235 in a middle class Italian family. From an early age his ambition was to become a cardinal and a member of the Sacred College which chose the Popes for the Roman Catholic Church. Once he realized his ambition, he persuaded the weak and inexperienced Pope Celestine V to renounce his position and return to the monastery.

Benedict speedily persuaded his fellow cardinals to elect him as pope and in 1235 Benedict became Pope Boniface VIII. He then used one quarter of Rome's revenue to purchase land for his own Gaetani family. He sold church offices and indulgences to amass his own personal wealth.

Benedict showed much more interest in politics than in spiritual matters. He desired to become the supreme authority in Europe and began warring with King Philip IV of France. In 1302 Pope Boniface VIII issued the bull *Unam Sanctam* which proclaimed the Pope to be the earthly ruler over all Christians. But paper declarations are different from actual realizations on the ground. His church rival arranged for his capture, leading to his death.

CONCLUSION

Thank God that the moral lapses of churches reported in the newspapers are not reflective of all churches. Many, many Christian leaders are faithful servants of God. They serve sacrificially. Many, many lay-Christians live Christ-honoring lives that serve as beacons of light in their communities.

But corruption in the nation and churches can only decline if more and more lay Christians would live exemplary faithful Christian lives wherever they are immersed in society: in positions of government, businesses, schools and elsewhere. Honest, hard-working, selfless and morally upright Christians can make a difference, and newspaper correspondents will take notice. Corruption will decrease dramatically and Jesus Christ will be glorified rather than vilified when Christians live for Christ in society.

Christians are nurtured within congregations where the Word of God is taught in the power of the Holy Spirit. But corruption in the nation declines only when those same mature Christians are living for Christ faithfully when working in society. Whatever your vocation, be honest and trustworthy, faithful and hardworking, loving and morally pure in heart.

4

CASE STUDY OF
THE CHURCH IN CORINTH

A study of the apostolic church in Corinth helps us understand the solution to the moral problems facing churches today.

During the first century of the Christian era Corinth was a Roman colony, one of the wealthiest and most influential cities in the Roman Empire. Her walls measured six miles in circumference. Sea traffic between the western Mediterranean Sea and the East contributed to her wealth and cosmopolitan nature. It attracted not only material wealth, but diverse religious traditions and pagan vices.

Paul's strategy in church planting was to visit urban centers with large Jewish populations because the Gospel must first be preached to the Jews, and then to the Gentiles (Ro 1:16). During his second missionary journey, some twenty years after the death, resurrection and ascension of Jesus Christ, Paul walked 46 miles from Athens to Corinth which had a large Jewish population and a synagogue.

Numbers of Jews were converted to faith in Jesus as the Messiah like Crispus, the ruler of the synagogue, but most converts were Gentiles. The Lord appeared to Paul in a vision and urged him not to be afraid, but to continue preaching. He remained in Corinth for eighteen months (Ac 18:11).

By the time Paul left Corinth a sizeable congregation of believers had formed, mostly Gentiles who lacked the moral teachings which the Jews had learned through the Old Testament Scriptures.

Leaving Corinth, Paul's next stop on his second missionary journey was Ephesus where he remained for three years (Ac 20:14), "*so that all the residents of Asia* [the Roman Province] *heard the word of the Lord, both Jews and Greeks*" (Ac 19:10). During that time in Ephesus he wrote an unknown letter to the Corinthians (1 Co 5:9), followed by 1 Corinthians. A year later, while ministering in Macedonia, Paul wrote 2 Corinthians to this church which had many problems and a complicated relationship with Paul.

He addressed the Corinthian church as "*those sanctified in Christ Jesus, called to be saints.*" He rejoiced "*because of the grace of God*" given to them and he called them "*brothers*" (1 Co 1:1-4, 10). Every person, born-again by the Spirit of God, is set apart (sanctified) in Christ and declared righteous (*"saints,"* and *"holy"* before God). This is the *position* of all believers in Christ. But Christians must continue to grow into the likeness of Christ and become increasingly holy in *practice* (an ongoing process of sanctification – becoming more holy in practice).

Nevertheless, these born again Christians were not *"spiritual people,"* but *"people of the flesh, as infants in Christ"* (1 Co 3:1). The Corinthian church was a troubled church with many moral failures. From this letter we can learn valuable lessons of how a church can and should become holy in their lives with a vibrant testimony throughout the nation.

Following is my analysis of the moral failures in the Corinthians church.

1. **Egotism produced divisions**
   a. **Leadership struggles** (1:17b – 4:21).
   b. **Social snobbery** (8:1 – 10:33).
   c. **Selfish ambition** (12:1 – 14:4).
2. **Lust of the flesh contaminated** (5:1 – 13; 6:12 – 20).
3. **Lust of the eyes became idolatrous** (6:1-6).

In this analysis egotism looms large and is found throughout the Corinthian church. This "Me First" attitude is even a motivating factor behind lust of the flesh and lust of the eyes.

The English word, "ego," is derived from the Latin word, *"ego,"* meaning "I." Hence egotism refers to self-centeredness, self-praise, self-admiration, selfishness, self-assertion, arrogance and boasting. In other words, egotism is <u>pride</u>. Egotism is all about "me." Putting "me" before God and others.

Idolatry is the worship of idols. We usually think of idols as images made of wood or precious metals. According to the New Testament, however, idolatry is loving any object or desire supremely more than God, and thus usurping the place of the living God who alone is to be worshipped and obeyed. Therefore, egotism, that is, "Me First," is idolatry (Eph 5:5).

Pope Gregory the Great around A.D. 600 suggested that all sin could be traced back to "Seven Cardinal Sins," later called "Seven Deadly Sins" (pride, lust, envy, greed, gluttony, anger, sloth). The first and deadliest of these seven sins is pride (egotism) with all other sins springing from pride.

It is natural, therefore, that egotism is found at the heart of every moral failure among the Christians in Corinth. Following are the moral failures of the Corinthian church and Paul's instructions to revolve those failures.

EGOTISM PRODUCED DIVISIONS

Divisions are common today in local church congregations and denominations. The causes of these divisions are varied, but they are almost always motivated by egotism ("Me First," that is, pride).

Egotism produced leadership struggles (1:10 – 4:21).

Most leadership struggles in churches today are caused by individuals who overtly or covertly campaign before an election, sometimes using bribery, night meetings and slander. The problem in Corinth was different.

These young believers divided themselves by showing loyalty to different leaders: *Paul*, the founding missionary/apostle of the church in Corinth; *Apollos*, the brilliant orator and astute teacher who followed Paul as the church leader in Corinth; *Peter*, the highly respected apostle to the Jews; and *Christ*, the Lord and Savior who is the Head of the Body of Christ (1 Co 1:10-14).

We all have our favorites. Some pastors are superb teachers, others are extraordinary evangelists, and still others are more personable and likeable.

The problem arises when we gossip with one another about our favorites or the ones we dislike. Unity is broken when groups coalesce around different leaders. Without unity church fellowship breaks down. Instead of focusing on worship and ministry, believers fall into factional arguments.

Paul called the Corinthian believers "*infants in Christ*." They were carnal Christians ("*people of the flesh*") and not spiritual because they "*behave only in a human way*." They were filled with "*jealousy and strife*" (1 Co 3:1-3 ESV).

Solution: Paul appealed for unity: "*stop arguing among yourselves. Let there be real harmony so there won't be divisions in the church. I plead with you to be of one mind, united in thought and purpose*" (1 Co 1:10).

This is a similar plea given to the church in Philippi where divisions had also developed. "*...make me truly happy by agreeing wholeheartedly with each other; loving one another, and working together with one heart and purpose*" (Php 2:2).

This is easier said than done. We may know what is right, but to see all believers behaving in unity is not easy. For unity to prevail in the local congregation, Christians must embrace two truths which Paul outlines:

Embrace Jesus Christ crucified as your wisdom and power (1 Co 1:17 – 2:5; 3:1 – 4). The first truth is Christ crucified. Wherever human beings co-mingle, they have different opinions. This is natural, and diversity has many advantages as long as people can all agree on the major issues. We learn from one another and can profit from those with different opinions. When Christians interact humbly and lovingly, they grow in their understanding. _"As iron sharpens iron, a friend sharpens a friend"_ (Pr 2:17). No one has a claim of knowing everything. We all need each other.

But when egotistical, self-centered church members and leaders insist on their own viewpoint, divisions occur. To overcome disunity Christians must become Christ-centered, becoming crucified with Christ. They must embrace this truth and embody Christ crucified in their lives. This abolishes the egotism of Christians which so often sullies the Church.

Paul's first point in resolving disunity was to remind the Corinthians that his emphasis in preaching was Christ crucified, not eloquent wisdom.

"Christ did not send me to baptize but to preach the gospel, and not with words of eloquent wisdom, lest the cross of Christ be emptied of its power" (1 Co 1:17 ESV; compare 1 Co 1:17 – 2:16).

Before preaching in Corinth, Paul had visited Athens, preaching and reasoning with the Greeks on Mars Hill. The Greeks with their language, philosophy, architecture and democratic form of government are the ancestors of western civilization. They prided themselves in their human wisdom and eloquent speech.

Paul had witnessed the Athenian arrogance first hand. In their pride they rejected the Gospel. Only a few Gentiles were converted in Athens and no church is recorded.

When Paul arrived in Corinth he boldly proclaimed Christ crucified on the cross in payment for the sins of humans. Heralding a crucified Christ as the Savior is total folly in human reasoning. For unbelievers the cross is a sign of weakness and foolishness. The Jews and others demand miraculous signs and wonders which demonstrate power, while the Greeks and others demand eloquent wisdom and philosophical sophistry.

But in God's sight, and in reality, the Gospel is the power of God that alone can save the lost (Ro 1:16). Only Christ crucified, not human power or wisdom, can rescue men from the dominion of Satan and transfer them to the kingdom of God's Son.

The cross of Christ is divine wisdom because it displays the glory of God's righteousness and grace. A just and righteous God cannot cancel our debt of sin without payment. Jesus is the Lamb of God who bore our sin, dying in our place as sinners. The cross, however, not only reflects the glory of a holy God, it also demonstrates the grace, mercy and lovingkindness of God who sovereignly grants forgiveness to sinners who repent and trust in Christ.

Only mature Christians understand God's wisdom because God has revealed it to them by his Spirit (1 Co 2:6, 10). *"We who have the Spirit understand these things, but others can't understand us at all...for we have the mind of Christ"* (1 Co 2:15, 16).

Humility comes when we embrace God's power and wisdom found in the Gospel. The Gospel strikes a lethal blow to the egotism springing from spiritually carnal and immature Christians. Only humility can unite people with diverse opinions. *"Not my will but your will be done,"* Jesus prayed.

Follow the example of Jesus Christ crucified as your wisdom and power (1 Co 3:5 – 4:21). Paul now addresses the leadership problem directly: *"Who is Apollos, and who is Paul, that we should be the cause of such quarrels? ...we are **only servants**"* (1 Co 3:5; 4:1). These Corinthian believers were puffed up, favoring one leader over another. They did not understand that leaders are mere servants. Church leaders become arrogant when they think of themselves as "big men," not as servants of God.

God gives to each believer particular gifts for church leadership, but no one has all the gifts in the same measure – preaching skills, teaching skills, evangelizing skills, counselling skills, inter-personal relationship skills, organizing and administrative skills, to name just a few. Some are gifted more and others less. Christians are very limited. They are dependent on God, who gifts them. Leaders should not try to be what they are not, emulating some popular, charismatic leader. That leads to hypocrisy and conceit.

What *is* required of all church leaders is that they are found faithful and trustworthy. God will not judge church leaders because they are not as gifted as others, but they will be judged if they are lazy, dishonest, and unfaithful in using their spiritual gifts for God's glory alone.

The tendency of Christians is to pass judgment on leaders, criticizing and critiquing them as if Christians were their judges. The tendency of

Christian leaders is to insulate themselves from their followers and act as if they know it all. Paul admonishes the Corinthian Christians:

"So be careful not to jump to conclusions before the Lord returns as to whether or not someone is faithful. When the Lord comes, he will bring our deepest secrets to light and will reveal our private motives. And then God will give to everyone whatever praise is due" (1 Co 4:5).

Becoming a Christ-like Christian leader requires the new birth by the Holy Spirit, followed by growth in the likeness of Christ, humbly crucified. Jesus Christ is not only our Savior, but our role model as Paul taught the Philippians who had their own church divisions:

"Don't be selfish; don't live to make a good impression on others. Be humble, thinking of others as better than yourself... **Your attitude should be the same that Christ Jesus had**. *Though he was God, he did not demand and cling to his rights as God. He made himself nothing; he took the humble position of a slave and appeared in human form. And in human form he obediently humbled himself even further by dying a criminal's death on a cross. Because of this, God raised him up to the heights of heaven and gave him a name that is above every other name, so that at the name of Jesus every knee will bow, in heaven and on earth and under the earth, and every tongue will confess that Jesus Christ is Lord, to the glory of God the Father"* (Php 2:3 – 11).

Nothing more needs to be said beyond this! Jesus Christ, the eternal Son of God, humbled himself by becoming a bondservant. God exhorts all disciples of Jesus Christ to have the same mind of humility. What needs to be done is not more exhortation or explanation, but obedience. Christians are expected to be faithful servants with humility toward God and others.

And yet we find Bible School and College graduates, who were taught the Scriptures and mentored in spiritual formation, becoming "Big Men." They graduate with seemingly humble, servant-like attitudes, only to be found years later as unfaithful. They become "Big Men" who lord it over others. They use their office to enrich themselves. They rig the elections to ensure their own reelection. They live for the "now" (prestige, honor and status) and forget their responsibility to please their Lord and Savior.

They forget the future Judgment Seat of Christ when they shall give an account of their lives before the Judge of all the earth. We have a saying, "There are two things you cannot escape: death and paying taxes." Better said, "No one can escape death or final judgment." It surely is coming. *"...it is destined that each person dies only once and after that comes judgment"* (Heb 9:27). Blessed is that Christian who lives his life with that in view.

Egotism produced social snobbery (8:1 – 10:33)

Living in the city of Corinth, Christians were confronted with pagan beliefs and practices in every aspect of their culture including the market place. Corinthians, who desired to purchase meat, visited the open air market where they could buy meat which most likely had been first offered to idols in the temple.

"Strong" Christians knew that there is only one God and that idols are lifeless objects with no real spiritual existence. Idols cannot contaminate food. The "strong" bought the meat in the market and ate it freely without feeling any guilt. But "weak" Christians believed that eating such meat was tantamount to participating in idolatry. Their consciences bothered them when they ate it. They were offended by Christians who ate meat sacrificed to idols.

The result was schism within this small band of Christians. "Strong" Christians looked down on the "weak" Christians in social snobbery. The "weak" Christians passed judgment on the "strong." This was not conducive to unity.

Solution: Paul agrees with the "strong" Christians in their beliefs. Believers in Christ should feel free to eat meat offered to idols if their consciences do not bother them. They are not bound by rules and regulations that are not found in Scripture. Legalism with extra-biblical mandates undermines the freedom we have in Christ.

But Paul warns that "knowledge puffs up." "Strong" Christians are in danger of egotism, placing self before others. Instead of pleasing self by eating meat offered to idols, "strong" Christians should be concerned for the welfare of others.

Yes, *"all things are lawful"* as Corinthian Christians said. Christians are free to engage in activities that are not specifically condemned by Scripture, *"but not all things are helpful." "Not all things build up."* The ambition of Christians should not be to do everything and anything which is not forbidden in Scripture. Their ambition should be twofold:

Seek the good of others, not your own good (1 Co 10:23, 24). Human beings by nature are self-centered. Putting self to be first is natural. Pleasing self instead of others is what all human beings do, but this should not be true of Christians. Their ambition in life should be to love others, help others, seek the well-being of others and live for others. This contributes to unity. As Paul told the Philippians: "*Don't think only about your own affairs, but be interested in others, too, and what they are doing*" (Php 2:4).

Paul gave his own life as an example of someone who had rights, but gladly gave up his rights for the advancement of the Gospel (1 Co 9:1 – 23). He had the right to marry and take his wife with him on his missionary journeys like the apostle Peter, but Paul gave up that right for the sake of the Gospel. He had the right to be supported by the churches, but he gave up that right so that he would not burden his converts. Christians should not try to hold on to their rights (their Christian freedoms) at the expense of others.

Do all for the glory of God (1 Co 10:31-33). God's people are his treasured possession. Rescued from the dominion of Satan and brought into the kingdom of God's Son, Christians should seek to display the glory of God's amazing grace (Eph. 1:6, 14). Our entire life in eternity will be for God's glory. The same should be true now. "*Whatever you eat or drink or whatever you do, you must do all for the glory of God*" (1Co 10:31).

We do not have the same dilemma that the Corinthian Christians had. We don't worry about eating meat offered to idols. But we have many other issues which are not clearly forbidden or clearly commanded. Instead of seeking our own good, we need to seek the good of others. We need to live as if we are truly running the Christian race in order to win.

Egotism produced selfish ambition (12:1-14:40).

A custom arose in the early church of eating a meal together for fellowship before partaking of the Lord's Supper. This was called an Agape Feast (or Love Feast). But instead of showing genuine love, the wealthy ate their own food while the poor sat with none (1 Co 11:17-19; c.f. Jude 1:12). The Corinthian Christians had become divided between the wealthy and the poor. Class snobbery can be as bad as racial animosity. These Christians lacked the agape love which should distinguish them from unbelievers.

Furthermore, when they gathered for worship, their self-love was again demonstrated by competing with one another, trying to show off their spiritual gifts (1 Co 12-14). God graciously gives to each believer spiritual gifts for the purpose of building up the Body of Christ. No one is left empty without any gift. Compared to a human body, the Body of Christ has members that are more prominent than others. The eyes gain more attention than the feet, the mouth more than a finger. Yet each body-part is needed.

God is the one who decides which spiritual gifts are given to each believer. *"It is the one and only Holy Spirit who distributes these gifts. He alone decides which gift each person should have"* (1 Co 12:11). Christians do not choose their own spiritual gifts. They only cultivate and develop the gifts God has given.

Just as salvation is by grace, so the impartation of spiritual gifts is by grace. These gifts are not meant for personal prestige or status. They are intended to edify the Body. God put the Body together in such a way that harmony is produced with each member caring for the others. When one member suffers, everyone suffers. Each believer is necessary (1 Co 12:25f).

The problem in Corinth, however, was that those with the more spectacular gifts, like speaking in tongues, magnified their gifts. They elevated themselves above the others. Pride/egotism led to division between members with differing gifts.

Solution: The solution to selfish ambition and self-promotion is genuine, Christ-like love. Paul inserts in the midst of his discussion of spiritual gifts the famous "love chapter" of the Bible. He transitions into the "love chapter" with these words: *"...earnestly desire the higher gifts* [i.e. prophecy]. *And I will show you a still more excellent way"* (1 Co 12:30c, 31 ESV).

Paul encourages Christians to *"earnestly desire higher gifts,"* but more importantly, they should desire to use those gifts with a spirit of love. The "more excellent way" than "earnestly desiring the higher gifts" is the use of those gifts with a spirit of love.

Exercising spiritual gifts is useless, and without any profit, if they are not used in a spirit of love for others. Christian love is **patient** and **kind**. Stating the further characteristics of love in the positive, we find that agape love is **generous** (*"not jealous"*), **humble** (*"not boastful"*), **modest** (*"not proud"*), **courteous** (*"not rude"*), **unselfish** (*"does not demand its own way"*), **good tempered** (*"not irritable"*), **forgiving** (*"keeps no record of when it has been wronged"*), **sincere** (*"never glad about injustice"*), **gracious** (*"rejoices whenever the truth wins out"*), **confident** (*"never gives up"*), and **enduring** (*"always hopeful and endures through every circumstance"*).

What dramatic changes would take place in every church if Christians loved one another like this, being patient with others, kind, humble, courteous, unselfish, good tempered, forgiving and genuinely sincere. Our churches would be transformed.

LUST OF THE FLESH CONTAMINATED

Corinth was a wealthy city with three ports and a population of 200,000 free citizens and hundreds of thousands of slaves, and it was unashamedly immoral. Though polytheistic, their greatest devotion was given to Aphrodite, the goddess of love. Her carvings portrayed her as a naked woman. She had three sanctuaries in the city, the most famous built on the top peak of the Acrocorinth overlooking the city. It was celebrated throughout Greece because of the 1,000 temple prostitutes, both men and women. Because of these prostitutes the city was crowded with visitors, and it grew rich.

Greek converts to Jesus Christ from this pagan city no doubt carried much of their cultural baggage with them. Corinthian Christians thought, "*I am allowed to do anything*" (1 Co 6:12). They believed that if God gave them a sexual urge, that meant they could gratify that desire even as they satisfied their hunger (1 Co 6:13).

But Paul argued that our bodies were not made for sexual immorality; they were meant for the Lord. In fact, the Christian's body is the temple of the Holy Spirit. "*Should a man take his body which belongs to Christ, and join it to a prostitute? Never! And don't you know that if a man joins himself to a prostitute, he becomes one body with her? ...Run away from sexual sin! ...You do not belong to yourself for God bought you with a high price*" (1 Co 6:15-20).

The Corinthian Christians tolerated and even applauded immorality that was not even practiced by the Greek pagans. A Christian man actually lived in sin with his father's wife (1 Co 5:1ff). Though only one Christian sinned in this way, the Christian congregation *tolerated* the sin. In fact, they were proud of this! Paul lamented: "*How terrible that you should boast about your spirituality, and yet you let this sort of thing go on*" (1 Co 5:6).

Incest with the wife of a man's father was uncommon in Greece, though the city of Corinth was plagued with other sins: "*idol worshipers, adulterers, male prostitutes, homosexuals, thieves, greedy people, drunkards, abusers and swindlers*" (1 Co 6:9-10). There was a time when some of the Corinthian Christians had engaged in those practices, but now their sins had been washed away and they were set apart for God.

Apparently, a crazy idea was passed around: "*I am allowed to do anything.*" This was backed up by a saying: "*Food for the stomach, and the stomach is for food*" (1 Co 12-13). But Paul warned them: "*Run away from sexual sin! ...You must honor God with your body*" (1 Co 6:18-20).

Solution: Paul admonished them to call a meeting of the church and expel the man from the assembly. "*...cast this man out of the church and into Satan's hands so that his sinful nature will be destroyed and he himself will be saved when the Lord returns...Remove this wicked person from among you so that you can stay pure*" (1 Co 5:5, 7).

Delivering this flagrant sinner "into Satan's hands" probably means expelling him from the assembly of believers and casting him into the world which is Satan's realm. The Greek word translated, *sinful nature*, is *sarx* (meaning "flesh"). This Greek word refers not only to the lower, sinful nature, but also the human body. Probably, Paul here recognizes that sexual sins frequently cause physical disease (Sexually Transmitted Disease - STD). The prayer is that expulsion from the Christian assembly and suffering the physical consequences of his sin will bring him to repentance.

Excommunicating a Christian may seem extreme and uncaring, but the purpose is very noble: to maintain purity of the church – "*so you can stay pure.*" Sin that requires extreme measures of excommunication are scandalous, deliberate and persistent sins which remain unrepented. Such sin becomes a reproach on the Lord, and if allowed to continue, will compromise the testimony of the church.

The purpose of church discipline is not only to maintain purity among the saints, but to restore the sinner, to shame him or her into acknowledging wrongdoing followed by repentance – that "*he himself will be saved when the Lord returns.*"

Church discipline is sadly lacking in many churches today. Sin is tolerated. This destroys the testimony of the church and allows the sin to spread within the fellowship.

The right way to discipline is outlined by the Lord in Matthew 18:15-17.

First, go to the believer in private, and lovingly confront him with his or her sin and urge them to repent and cease from that sin. This should be done gently and humbly (Gal 6:1). If he or she repents, no need exists to excommunicate the believer.

Secondly, if the sinner is rebuked in private, but refuses to repent, *"take one or two others with you and go back again, so that everything you say may be confirmed by two or three witnesses."* Charges of sin should not be made apart from a thorough investigation and uncontestable evidence, so that *"every charge may be established by the evidence of two or three witnesses"* (ESV). These witnesses must confirm that a particular sin has been committed and that the believer has refused to repent. If he or she repents, no need exists to excommunicate the believer.

Thirdly, if the believer still does not acknowledge his sin and repent, the sinner should be brought before the whole church including the elders. The case must be fully explained to the congregation with sufficient evidence to remove any questions or doubt. If the sinner refuses to appear in person before the congregation, the report of his sin should be brought before the assembly.

Before church discipline takes place, the church should be absolutely certain that the accused brother has actually sinned and continues to sin as the accusers say, and that the accused refuses to repent. Lest there be bias or unfair accusations by one person, two or three others should confirm the facts. Church discipline is necessary, but potentially explosive. Excommunication should not take place unless there is sufficient, and unmistakable evidence that the sin has taken place.

"If the church decides you are right, but the other person won't accept it, treat that person as a pagan or a corrupt tax collector." It is only at this point, if the person continues to be unrepentant, that he or she should be excommunicated. He is no longer permitted to take the Lord's Super and is considered a "pagan," that is, outside the Christian fellowship (Mt 18:17).

Fourthly, the purpose of this church discipline is not final rejection but restoration upon repentance. Though the accused is outside the Christian fellowship, the disciplined person should be loved, and lovingly urged to repent. In Paul's second canonical letter to the Corinthians, he alludes to another case where discipline was exercised and a person excommunicated (2 Co 2:5-11). In that case, Paul decided that the discipline was sufficient and he should be restored lest he become *"so discouraged that he won't be able to recover. Now show him that you still love him"* (2 Co 2:8).

Church discipline is complex and difficult and cannot be treated thoroughly in this book. But what must be stressed is that: (1) church discipline is very important to maintain purity within the congregation and provide a sterling testimony of holy living before the world; but (2) church discipline must be done wisely, carefully and lovingly with the goal of repentance and restoration. Too many churches either neglect church discipline or carry it out unwisely with animosity. Church discipline can be an explosive problem, so don't let sin grow and fester.

LUST OF THE EYES IS IDOLATRY

Paul lamented that when a Corinthian Christian had "*something against another Christian,*" the accused was taken to the Corinthian city court (1 Co 6:1). It would appear that this "*something*" had to do with money or property for Paul later speaks of being "*cheated.*" The Greek word means "*to defraud, rob, despoil.*" This accused Christian obtained money or property illegally from a brother or sister in the congregation by deception (1 Co 6:7). Paul was appalled.

Here we want to discuss more carefully the problem of greed that is the root cause of unjust defrauding. Whenever a person illegally snatches something of value from another it is due to greed. Paul indicates that Corinthian believers before their conversion had been guilty of greed, and this sin continued in the church after their conversion (1 Co 5:10-11). Lamentably, greed continues to be an unrelenting problem among Christians to this very day.

Envy is resentful feelings aroused by the possessions of someone else. *Envy* leads inevitably to *coveting* what someone else has. Envy and covetousness are major sins.

Of the Ten Commandments given to the children of Israel at Mt. Sinai, nine referred to external behavior (killing, lying, adultery etc.) Only one dealt with internal attitudes and desires, namely, "*Do not covet...*" (Ex 20:17). Envy, leading to covetousness, has led to class warfare, stealing, cattle raids, violence and military conflict.

Luke tells of a man who asked Jesus to intervene on his behalf and compel his brother to share his inheritance. Possibly, he was the younger brother who felt defrauded of his heritage. Instead of entering into a legal dispute, Jesus went straight to the root problem – covetousness and greed

– saying: *"Beware! Don't be greedy for what you don't have. Real life is not measured by how much we have"* (Lk 12:15).

Greed, so common among Christians and non-Christians, is on the same level as murder and adultery. In fact, one could argue that greed is far worse because greed is idolatry, the worship of material possessions.

"Don't be greedy for the good things of this life, for that is idolatry. God's terrible anger will come upon those who do such things" (Col 3:5-6).

Murder and adultery are sins against fellow human beings, a failure to love your neighbor as yourself. Greed is failing to love God with all your heart, soul, strength and mind, for it defies the will of God, yearning for earthly things contrary to God's will.

A choice must be made. Either you worship and serve God, or you worship and serve your own lust for things. As Jesus said:

"No one can serve two masters. For you will hate one and love the other, or be devoted to one and despise the other. You cannot serve both God and money" (Mt 6:4).

Perhaps a word should be said to distinguish between unlawful desires and lawful desires. Greed is what we call "inordinate" or "excessive" desires. These desires are all-absorbing and all-controlling. Such desires consume the mind and supplant the will of God as Lord. Incessant craving for earthly possessions displaces worship of God, love of family and faithfulness to God's holy law. Therefore, greed is idolatry.

Lawful desires are not all-consuming, but subservient to God's will. Desiring a new dress or shirt, a newer and better car is not greedy whenever submitted to God in prayer, seeking his will. Those who make known to God their desires, and wait upon the Lord to guide and provide according to his will, are not greedy. Excessive desire for material gain destroys contentment. Wealth can never replace joy and peace.

"Now there is great gain in godliness with contentment, for we brought nothing into the world, and we cannot take anything out of the world. But if we have food and clothing, with these we will be content. But those who desire to be rich fall into temptation, into a snare, into many senseless and harmful desires that plunge people into ruin and destruction. For the love of money is a root of all kinds of evil. It is through this craving that some have wandered away from the faith and pierced themselves with pangs" (1 Ti 6:6-10 ESV).

Solution: Corinthian Christians cheated each other, defrauding fellow believers. In response the victims took these cheats to court, seeking justice from the pagans (1 Co 6:1-8).

Paul was appalled. How can Christians take their own legal disputes to pagan courts when Christians will judge angels? Churches should set up their own court system to resolve ordinary disagreements. Certain denominations have done this. The tragedy is that many have not. They wash their dirty linen in the public and bring disgrace to the Name of Christ.

Today newspaper articles spread abroad the disgraceful news of greed, theft and the misappropriation of funds by pastors, bishops, church officers and members. This is disgraceful! Instead of taking such issues to state courts, churches should exercise discipline and adjudicate disputes through church councils and internal courts.

CONCLUSION

Egotism (self-centeredness and pride) caused havoc in the Corinthian church by dividing the believers into many factions – leadership struggles, strong versus the weak, the rich versus the poor. Egotism lay behind the prejudice which Corinthians had towards others – social snobbery, not dissimilar to clan, tribal, racial, and class prejudice so common today. Pride lies behind every problem troubling the church including their greed and immorality.

The true (invisible) Church is the Body of Christ. As such the believers should live honorable, Christ-centered lives. When they do not, the Name of Christ is reproached. Instead of glorifying Christ, they dishonor the Lord and disgrace themselves.

Our first parents, Adam and Eve, are the ones who thrust the whole human race into the present human condition. The sequence of Eve's sin is instructive. Satan first raised doubts about God's integrity and goodness, and then he lied: "'*You won't die' the serpent hissed. 'God knows that your eyes will be opened when you eat it. You will become just like God, knowing everything, both good and evil*'" (Ge 3:4-5).

The heart of sin is idolatry – removing God from his throne and replacing God with self. This is nothing more than egotism (pride and self-centeredness – "Me First").

"*So when the woman saw that the tree was good for food* [lust of the flesh], *and it was a delight to the eyes* [lust of the eyes], *and that the tree was to be desired to make one wise* [pride of life], *she took of its fruit and ate, and she also gave some to her husband who was with her, and he ate"* (Ge 3:6-7 ESV).

A careful examination in the life of Christ shows that the same pattern of temptation prevailed when Satan tempted Jesus with lust of the flesh, lust of the eyes and the pride of life (Mt 4:1-10; cf. 1 Jn 2:15-17). But Jesus overcame by trusting God, hiding God's Word in his heart and obeying God's Word.

For the Church of Jesus Christ to be the light and salt in society, _every_ believer should prayerfully seek God's help to submit to the lordship of Jesus Christ, instead of being ego-centric. Christian believers have an important part to play in being lights in their community – at work and school, in the market, and even holding political office in government. By living honest lives with integrity, and by offering loving, selfless service, Christians can restrain corruption in society (being salt) and show the way for transparent, honorable and godly governance (being light) in the nation.

Church members also need to ensure that their church leaders are Christ-centered and not self-centered. They need to make the following words their daily prayer.[1]

"Not I, but Christ be honored, loved, exalted.
Not I, but Christ be seen, be known and heard;
Not I, but Christ in every look and action;
Not I, but Christ in every thought and word.

Oh, to be saved from myself, dear Lord,
Oh, to be lost in Thee,
Oh, that it may be no more I,
But Christ that lives in me.

Christ, only Christ, no idle word e'er falling,
Christ, only Christ, no needless bustling sound;
Christ, only Christ, no self-important bearing,
Christ, only Christ, no trace of "I" be found."

---

[1] Lyrics of song, *"Not I but Christ,"* written by of Ada Anne Whiddington

BUILDING BLOCKS FOR
A VIBRANT CHURCH
Part One: Growth into Maturity

A clear-eyed view of Christian history shows that in general the Church in the past 2,000 years has been no more faithful to God than the nation of Israel. Furthermore, the social problems in Africa are not essentially any different from the social problems that plague the West and elsewhere.

But this _need not be_. It _should not be_. Through Christ and the working of the Holy Spirit, Christians can live in obedience. Wherever a vibrant church with faithful, obedient Christians is found, a positive influence occurs in their spheres of influence. Society is enriched and bettered through the lives of Christians who live according to God's Word.

In this chapter we seek to present briefly the building blocks for the formation of a vibrant church. These building blocks should not be thought of as separate bricks, unrelated to each other. Many overlap. Repetition occurs. Neither should they be thought of as a roadmap, moving necessarily from one point to another toward the final destination. There is a definite progression, but God moves uniquely with each of his children.

Just as bricks interrelate in a brick-house, interconnecting and building on lower rows of bricks, so these building blocks intersect and overlap one another. What we can say is that when all these building blocks are in place within each Christian and in each congregation, a transformation will take place not only in the local church, but in society around it.

What is desperately needed is a prayer movement by God's people, confessing their sins and seeking God's merciful outpouring of his Spirit.

"Then if my people who are called by my name will humble themselves and pray and seek my face and turn from their wicked ways, I will hear from heaven and will forgive their sins and heal their land" (2 Ch 7:14).

What is here presented is not some new discovery. The truth laid out is basic teaching with which all Christians should be acquainted. What is needed is a deep and profound movement of the Holy Spirit to bring about change. What is needed is serious commitment by Christians to love and serve God with all their hearts, souls, strength and minds.

1. COUNTING THE COST

Becoming a disciple of Jesus Christ is costly. Sadly, the offer of salvation is often presented as a cheap Gospel. Just believe and you will be saved. The Scripture actually says: "Believe on the _Lord Jesus_ and you will be saved" (Ac 16:31). Thank God that Jesus died on the cross for our sins and through repentance and faith we are freely and graciously saved from condemnation. We cannot save ourselves. Salvation does not depend on good works (Eph 2:8-9). By simple faith we are saved.

But when we cast ourselves on Jesus and ask him to become our Savior, _he also becomes our Lord._ We submit to his lordship in our lives. We are no longer our own for we have been bought with a price (1 Co 6:19-20).

We read that great crowds followed Jesus who were amazed by his miracles. _"He turned around and said to them, 'If you want to be my follower you must love me more than your own father and mother, wife and children, brothers and sisters – yes, more than your own life. Otherwise, you cannot be my disciple"_ (Lk 14:26-27).

That is strong talk! Before deciding to follow Christ, you need to count the cost. Jesus continued with two illustrations. Before someone starts a building project, a wise person _first_ calculates whether he can afford to complete the building. Before an army general decides to confront an invading army, a wise general _first_ determines whether he has sufficient military strength to engage the enemy successfully.

Jesus concluded: _"So no one can become my disciple without giving up everything for me"_ (Lk 14:33). Our possessions and income now belong to the Lord who saved us. Our desires and plans are under his direction. Christ's will for our lives becomes our will as we submit to his lordship.

On another occasion an enthusiastic follower of Jesus blurted out: _"I will follow you no matter where you go."_ Amazing! What commitment that was! But Jesus cautions him. "Have you considered the cost?" Before making such commitment, a person must think through what you say.

Jesus responded: _"Foxes have dens to live in, and birds have nests, but I, the Son of Man, have no home of my own, not even a place to lay my head"_ (Lk 9:58).

Thank God for those who have made this commitment, following Jesus wherever he leads. I've seen many of God's servants sacrificing greatly to follow Jesus. While others lived in spacious, comfortable homes, they lived in functional accommodations which kept them dry during the rains, all for the Gospel's sake. Great will be their reward when they meet their Lord and hear his words: *"Well done, good and faithful servant."*

Jesus turned to another follower and said: *"Come, be my disciple."* Think of the privilege of this invitation! But this man paused and thought of what it would cost. He decided to follow Jesus *but first*, he said, *"let me return home and bury my father."* It is highly unlikely that his father had already died for the man would have been at home at that moment, attending to the affairs of burial. Jews considered proper burial highly important. More likely, the man wanted to return home and care for his aging father until he died. *Then* he would become a follower of Jesus.

Jesus replied: *"Let those who are spiritually dead care for their own dead. Your duty is to go and preach the coming of the Kingdom of God"* (Lk 9:60). The privilege of being called into the Christian ministry is awesome, but parents are often unwilling to submit their wills to God's will. They want their children to earn much money and become successful in this world. Young people also hesitate to surrender their lives to the Lord for fear of poverty and loss. But when we become Christ's disciples, our desires must be submitted to God's will. "Jesus is Lord of all or he is not Lord at all." Before becoming disciples of Christ, we should count the cost.

On another occasion Jesus said: *"If any of you wants to be my follower, you must give up your own way, take up your cross daily, and follow me. If you try to hang on to your life, you will lose it. But if you give up your life for my sake, you will save it"* (Lk 9:23-24).

Christians often wear a cross without recognizing its significance. Death by crucifixion was so excruciating that Roman citizens were rarely crucified, mostly for treason. But Jesus says that if you want to be a disciple of Jesus you must *"give up your own way and take up your cross daily."*

Each person's cross is shaped differently. Many throughout the world, more today than ever before, are called upon to suffer torture and even death for being a Christian. Many are thrown out of the family and counted as dead. Others are scorned, ridiculed and humiliated. Jesus denied himself when submitting to his Father's will and so must all of Christ's followers.

But consider the cost of choosing *not* to be a Christian! Jesus warned: *"And how do you benefit if you gain the whole world but lose your own soul in the process? Is anything worth more than your soul?"* (Mt 16:26).

2. BEING BORN AGAIN

Many call themselves "Christians" because they were been born into a Christian home, attend church, and live in a community that is nominally Christian. Unsaved youth think they are Christians because they've been invited to teach Sunday School. These are "cultural Christians," not "born again" Christians.

One night after dark, Nicodemus came to Jesus. He was a very religious man, a Pharisee, known for praying, fasting and being strict in keeping the Jewish law. Jesus bluntly told him: *"I assure you, unless you are born again, you can never see the Kingdom of God"* (Jn 3:3).

His strict religiosity was not good enough. Being good or trying to do good will not qualify anyone from entering the Kingdom of God. As Jesus said: *"Humans can reproduce only human life, but the Holy Spirit gives new life from heaven"* (Jn 3:6).

Cultural Christianity (i.e. nominal Christianity) is common. Each Christian and each Christian church needs continual renewal through the Holy Spirit because of the tendency to drift away from their first love of God. First generation Christians are usually vibrant believers who witness to their faith. But the second or third generation, without being born again, become nominal in their faith without any experience of the new birth.

This happened in Uganda years ago. Evangelical Anglican missionaries first preached the Gospel in Uganda in 1877. There was a remarkable response with many being saved. By some standards the Anglican Church was still thriving even in the early 20th century. Between 1921 and 1930 over 300 churches were planted. People flocked to the churches.

But spiritually the Church was dying. Drunkenness and immorality were common. Witchcraft was practiced by many Christians. Little difference could be found between Christians and non-Christians.

Historians date the East African Revival from 1936/1937 during the Diamond Jubilee of the founding of the Anglican Church in Uganda. Many were in united prayer for a movement of the Holy Spirit. Dr. Joe Church conducted a mission at Bishop Tucker Theological College in Mukono for students preparing for ministry. As he preached on sin, repentance, the new birth, separation from the world, the victorious life and the Holy Spirit, students were convicted of their sin. The result was the conversion of forty students who were transformed. They traveled throughout Uganda preaching. A great revival broke out among the churches with nominal Christians being born again and transformed.

According to Jesus, *"no one can enter the Kingdom of God without being born of water and the Spirit"* (Jn 3:5). This is explained in Titus 3:5. *"He saved us, not because of the good things we did, but because of his mercy. He washed away our sins and gave us a new life through the Holy Spirit."*

On the one hand, the new birth is supernaturally given from above. It involves the washing away of sins (symbolized by water baptism) and the impartation of new life – a work of the Holy Spirit. On the other hand, salvation requires a person to *repent of sin* and *trust in Christ* to forgive and save. Through faith we are declared righteous (Ro 3:19-20).

But there are two kinds of faith which can be illustrated. Jean-Francois Gravelet was famous in the 19th century for his ability to walk across tight ropes. In 1859 he thrilled thousands of spectators as he successfully walked across a tight rope over Niagara Falls between Canada and the U.S.A.

He then asked the crowd of thousands whether they believed he could carry a man on his back. The crowd agreed. Yes, *they believed that* he could do that. He then asked for a volunteer, but *no one trusted him* to do that.

Many *believe* the Gospel intellectually. They give mental assent to the Apostles Creed. Yes, they *believe that* Jesus died for them and saves them through faith. But they don't actually *trust in* Christ, they don't *rest on Jesus* to save them from damnation. They think they also must help in saving themselves. That is why the Bible says, *"Believe on the Lord Jesus Christ and you will be saved."*

We recognize that something is seriously wrong with humanity and ourselves. The core problem is that we are self-centered. We hurt others in order to benefit ourselves. We want our own way instead of God's way. We want to be masters of our own lives instead of submitting to God's will. This is what God says is "sin" and the wages of sin is death (Ro 6:23).

Since we are under God's judgment and unable to change our human nature, God did for us what we cannot do for ourselves. In love God gave his only Son, Jesus Christ, to pay our penalty for sin by dying on the cross in our place (Isa 53:1-12).

What each person must do to be saved is to be truly sorry for their sin and place their trust in Christ. God has no grandchildren. Christian parents do not give birth to Christian children. Each person must be born again.

3. BECOMING A LIVING SACRIFICE

The story is told of an evangelist who preached the Gospel to a gathering of American Indians many years ago. As he declared God's love for all peoples, the Indian chief stood up and said: "Me Indian chief give my bows and arrows and my hunting dogs to the Lord Jesus." But the evangelist replied, "The Lord doesn't want your hunting dogs, or bows and arrows."

Disappointed, the Indian chief returned to his seat. The evangelist continued to speak of sin and God's judgment, but also of God's love in sending his only Son, Jesus Christ, to pay for the penalty of our sins. The Indian chief arose again from his seat and exclaimed: "Me Indian chief give my wigwam (tent) and my wives to Jesus." But the evangelist replied that God was not interested in his wigwam and wives." Distressed and confused, he returned to his seat.

As the evangelist continued speaking of God's mercy and grace in providing a means eternal life for all sinners, the Indian chief arose one more time and said: "Me Indian chief give my body to the Lord Jesus. That is all I have." The evangelist replied, "That is what the Lord wants. He pleads with you to give your whole self, your body, soul and spirit."

This is exactly what Paul teaches in Romans. After explaining the riches of God's mercy and his marvelous plan of salvation through faith in Jesus Christ who died on the cross for sinners, Paul declares:

"And so, dear brothers and sisters, I plead with you to give your bodies to God. Let them be a living and holy sacrifice – the kind he will accept. When you think of what he has done for you, is this too much to ask?"

In the Old Testament we read that God offered the first sacrifice to clothe the shamefully sinful Adam and Eve with garments of skin. Later, he commanded Israel to offer sacrifices for their sins, explaining:

"I have given you the blood so you can make atonement for your sins. It is the blood, representing life, that brings atonement" (Lev 17:11). *"But it is impossible for the blood of bulls and goats to take away sins"* (Heb 10:4).

Jesus fulfilled the meaning of animal sacrifices. Jesus Christ became the Lamb of God, offering his body and blood to take away the sin of the world (Jn 1:20). Animal sacrifices are not needed (Heb 10:1-14). Jesus paid it all.

But now God pleads, begs and appeals with his people to offer their bodies as living sacrifices. Bloody sacrifices for sin were killed, but the sacrifices we make are living – a whole, long life of devotion to God.

Although God desires our whole selves to be given to him, he specifies our bodies. Why our bodies? Because it is with our bodies (eyes, mouth, hands, feet and mind) that we conduct ourselves, whether for God's glory or in disobedience to him.

Just as the lambs sacrificed in the Old Testament were without spot or blemish, even so our bodies should be lived with holiness unto the Lord. Our bodies should never be used for unclean purposes.

My parents led me to repent and trust Christ at the age of five. In my childlike way I trusted in the *Lord* Jesus Christ. But trusting in Christ and submitting my life to Christ's lordship is a growing and deepening experience that has continued throughout my life.

As a teenager I dedicated my life to the Lord and felt called to serve the Lord in Africa. After furthering my education, my wife and I sailed for Kenya. But every home assignment I returned to that very spot at the former Mizpah Grove Camp Meeting where I first dedicated my life to the Lord Jesus, and I rededicated my life to the Lord once again. Even when retirement came, before leaving Kenya, I rededicated my life to the Lord for retirement at a place on Kenya's coast called Mizpah where we slept the first night in Kenya. Yes, we should present our bodies as living sacrifices when we trust Christ as our Savior, but this is an ongoing process.

We face many challenges in life (financial, health, relationships, work temptation etc.) when our faith is tested. Our relationship with God should be such that day by day we surrender our lives to Lord because of God's mercies to us. Day by day we need to ask God for his grace to help us use our bodies only and always for God's glory.

Earlier Paul warned: "*Do not let any part of your body become a tool of wickedness*" (Ro 6:13). The verb really means: "*Do not go on letting your body parts become tools of wickedness.*" Born again Christians have all the resources needed to resist the temptation of using their bodies for ungodly purposes. With the Holy Spirit living within believers and praying at all times in the power of the Spirit, and using the armor of God, all believers can live holy lives (Eph 6:10-18).

Jesus Christ, God's only Son, offered his body as a sacrifice to pay for our salvation. Now we should offer our own bodies as living sacrifices in gratitude for all that Christ has done for us. When Christians do this daily, churches will become more Christ-like and our nations will be changed.

4. GROWING AS A CHRISTIAN DISCIPLE

Every family is thrilled when an infant is born into the home. We love babies. But if that baby remains a cute little baby, no one is happy. Babies are supposed to grow.

When someone is born again, he is in fact a baby Christian. He has eternal life, the blessed Holy Spirit dwells in him and he is indeed a child of God. But he knows little about how to live a Christian life. He has no experience of overcoming temptation and pleasing God. His prayer life is elementary and basic. The Bible is a relatively new book to him. He needs to grow.

The Greek word for "disciple" means "a learner." A disciple is a "pupil." The disciples of Jesus here on earth followed him in order to learn as he taught from place to place. A Christian disciple today is a pupil and follower of Jesus Christ as he or she learns from him through the Scriptures. The whole Bible is about Jesus Christ (Lk 24:25-27). Christians cannot grow into maturity and be all that God wants them to be without reading, studying, and meditating on the written Word of God.

The problem for many church members and attendees is twofold: Many are nominal or cultural Christians without any personal relationship with God; others are baby Christians, even though they professed faith in Christ decades ago. How does a Christian grow into spiritual maturity?

Essential is the reading, studying, memorizing and meditating on the Word of God. The Apostle Peter makes this clear: "*You must crave pure spiritual milk so that you can grow into the fullness of your salvation. Cry out for this nourishment as a baby cries for milk, now that you have had a taste of the Lord's kindness*" (1 Pe 2:3).

The reason why missionaries translate the Bible into the mother tongues of the peoples whom they evangelize, and the reason why they teach literacy for all believers is the need for every Christian to read their own Bibles for themselves. The reason why African church leaders supported and led the effort to prepare the *Africa Study Bible*[i] is to help Africans study and better understand the Scriptures.

The reason why medieval Christians became darkened in their Christian knowledge and living is because their church leaders were ignorant of biblical teaching. Depending on church traditions instead of biblical teachings, the Christian Church fell into gross error of spiritual darkness. Only when Martin Luther began reading, studying, and searching the Bible did he come to understand the way of salvation through grace alone and through faith alone in Christ, and thus launched the Protestant Reformation.

The purpose of reading, studying, memorizing and meditating on the Word of God is *not* to gain knowledge to pass a written test. It is to learn how to live a life that pleases God. As the Psalmist writes: "*I have hidden your word in my heart, that I might not sin against you*" (119:110).

The Apostle Paul makes this clear when writing to the Colossians:

"*And so, from the day we heard, we have not ceased to pray for you, asking that you may be filled with the knowledge of his will in all spiritual wisdom and understanding, so as to walk in a manner worthy of the Lord, fully pleasing to him, bearing fruit in every good work and increasing in the knowledge of God*" (Col 1:9-10 ESV).

This means three things: *First*, all literate Christians should own and read faithfully their Bibles in daily devotions. For Christians who are unable to read, there are audio recordings of the Bible available. From your reading and listening to Scripture, ask yourself several questions: (1) Is there a command to obey? (2) Is there an example to follow? (3) Is there a promise to claim? (4) Is there a sin to avoid? (5) Is there a principle to follow?[ii]

Second, all Christians should attend faithfully a Bible believing church with a pastor who preaches and teaches from the Word of God. In our day liberal churches doubt the authority of the Scriptures and the preachers do not expound and explain the Scriptures. Worship and fellowship with fellow disciples of Christ are essential for all Christians (Heb 10:25).

A log only keeps burning when lying with other logs. Try it! Several burning logs heaped together will continue to burn. Separate one log from the others and it will soon die out. In the same way, a Christian disciple needs to be with others to worship and learn together in order to keep the embers of faith growing.

Third, Christians should seek to study the Scriptures together in Bible study groups whenever such Bible studies are available. The more you know and understand of Scriptures and apply it to your own lives, the more you will grow and mature.

When churches are filled with mature Christian disciples, those churches become strong; and the more those Spirit filled Christians live for Christ in their communities, the less corruption will be found in the nation. Mature Christians who seek to obey Christ make the difference wherever they are.

5. ABIDING IN CHRIST

Jesus and his Twelve had been together in the Upper Room to celebrate the Passover meal (Jh 13-14). During the institution of Communion (the Lord's Supper), Satan entered into Judas Iscariot who had been with Jesus from the beginning. He suddenly arose and left the others in order to arrange his betrayal of Jesus; and it was night (Jn 13:23-30). After further teaching of the Eleven, Jesus said *"Come, let's be going"* (Jn 14:31).

Vineyards grew everywhere in the Holy Land. Possibly, pointing to vineyards on their way from Jerusalem to Gethsemane, Jesus taught a profound truth through an allegory about the vine.

The allegory spoke of two groups: branches that bear fruit and those which do not. These two branches are treated differently. The branches bearing fruit are pruned, but those not bearing fruit are cut off and burned.

From all outward appearances Judas was no different from the other eleven apostles. They had all been with Jesus for three years. But Judas ended up betraying Jesus in unbelief, while the other eleven remained faithful to Jesus to the point of even dying as martyrs. This allegory of the vineyard explains the difference.

The secret of bearing spiritual fruit is to "abide" in Jesus. The Greek word, *meno*, means to "remain," "dwell," "stay," "lodge," "abide" and "live." It appears ten times in 15:1-10 and is the primary emphasis of this passage. Just as a branch cannot continually live and bear fruit without a vital relationship with the vine, neither can a believer in Christ live and bear fruit without a continued, vital relationship with Christ. The vine provides the sap for the branch. Without sap the branch withers and dies.

There is a two directional flow of "remaining:" *"If you remain in me and my words remain in you, ask whatever you wish and it will be given you* (15:7 ESV)."[2] The living sap flowing from the vine into the branch is derived from Christ (15:4) and his Word (15:7). The requirement of the branch is to "remain" in the vine, namely, in Christ (15:1).

This reciprocal relationship involves both prayer and meditating on God's Word with obedience. Prayer and God's Word intertwine.

---

[2] God does not answer our prayers according to our desires, but only according to God's will. If we truly abide in Christ and his Word abides in us, our prayers will be according to his will and thus God will answer our prayers. We must interpret Scripture with Scripture. Answered prayer is according to God's will (1 Jn 5:14).

We have previously seen that spiritual growth into maturity depends on the reading, studying, memorizing and studying the Word of God. But this must be accompanied by prayerfully abiding in Christ. The Word of God and prayer are inseparable. We pray biblically as we are informed by Scripture which we hide in our hearts; and we learn spiritual truths from the Word as we prayerfully seek the illumination of the Holy Spirit. Prayer and meditating on Scripture go hand in hand.

The Scriptures teach: "*Keep on praying*" or "*Pray without ceasing*" (1 Th 5:16). How can we do this? We should be continually conscious of our total dependence on God. Hence we live in God's presence with faith and obedience. We thank God, rejoice in God, seek God's help and talk (pray) to God throughout the day. In this spirit of prayerfully relying on God we are abiding and dwelling in Christ. By this means the "sap" of God's grace flows into our very being.

Jesus, born of the Virgin Mary (fully human) and impregnated by the Holy Spirit (fully God), abode in the Vine throughout his earthly life. He prayed without ceasing. "*Jesus often withdrew to lonely places and prayed*" (Lk 5:16). He prayed at his baptism (Lk 3:21). He fasted and prayed for forty days in the wilderness prior to his ministry (Mt 4:1-2). Despite his busy schedule of ministry (morning, afternoon and evening), he arose in the morning while it was still dark and went to a solitary place to pray (Mk 1:35-37). Before he chose his Twelve Apostles he spent the whole night in prayer (Lk 6:12-13), and the night before his crucifixion he prayed so earnestly that his sweat was like drops of blood (Lk 22:39-46). He exhorted his disciples, "*Get up and pray. Otherwise temptation will overpower you.*"

Jesus left us an example of a deeply personal relationship with God. That relationship was maintained through prayer. As the God-Man, Jesus bore much fruit because he maintained his close relationship with his Father.

Salvation is by grace *alone*, through faith *alone* in Jesus Christ *alone*. We are born again from above, not through our own efforts any more than humans give birth to themselves.

But as children of God we are responsible to abide in the Vine (Jesus) through prayer in order to receive the "spiritual sap" from the vine. And we are responsible to meditate on Scripture so that God's Word is hidden in our hearts. The Spirit of God helps us to pray in ways we know not how, even as we immerse ourselves in the teachings of God's Word and learn how to pray in accordance with God's will.

6. UNDERSTANDING YOUR SALVATION

Witnessing to your faith should not wait until you have a deep understanding of salvation. Once you have received the Lord Jesus Christ as your Savior, you are naturally filled with the joy of your salvation – the knowledge that your sins have been forgiven and that you are now a child of God. You share with your family and friends of your new found faith.

But having a deeper understanding of salvation strengthens your ability to witness, and it strengthens your ability to resist temptation. According to African Christian leaders, many African believers fall back into African traditional practices when facing sickness and death because they do not understand the breadth, width, depth and height of their salvation. [iii]

We are GUILTY OF SIN: Adam and Eve were created sinless and given all good things to enjoy in life, but were given this command: "*You may freely eat any fruit in the garden except fruit from the tree of the knowledge of good and evil. If you eat of its fruit, you will surely die*" (Ge 2:16-17; Ro 3:23). Because of unbelief, they rebelled and disobeyed God.

Following their disobedience, (1) They died spiritually (and eventually died physically). (2) They became guilty before God, (3) fell under God's judgment and (4) their fellowship with God was broken. No longer subject to God's law, (5) they were enslaved to their own passions and evil desires in the dominion of Satan. Salvation is the reversal of this spiritual plight of human beings through faith alone in Jesus Christ alone and by grace alone.

GOOD NEWS: Because of God's love and grace, he sent his only Son, Jesus Christ, to die on the cross in the place of sinners to pay the penalty for sin. Salvation is offered to those who trust in Jesus as their Lord and Savior to reverse the sentence of death pronounced upon them (Ro 10:9f).

We are BORN AGAIN (REGENERATED): Everyone is born "*dead, doomed forever because of their many sins...But God is so rich in mercy, and he loved us so much, that even while we were dead because of our sins, he gave us life when he raised Christ from the dead*" (Eph 2:1,4-5). Though we were born once physically, we need to born again spiritually. The new birth is a mysterious event as the Spirit of God breathes new life into a spiritually dead person (Jn 3:1-15). Being born again is a supernatural event in which God moves into the hearts of sinners and regenerates them.

We are JUSTIFIED: That is, we are declared righteous before God – just as if we had never sinned. The term, "justified," is a word referring to an action taken in a court of law wherein an accused person is pronounced "just" and "innocent." Sinners are "pardoned" by grace through faith in Christ who paid for the penalty of sin on the cross (Ro 3:21-26).

We are SAVED from the penalty of sin: To be saved is to be rescued from the penalty of eternal death in hell pronounced on all sinners. We are saved from God's wrath. Salvation is all by grace through faith in Christ who alone paid for our penalty of sin (Eph 2:8-9). Nothing we do (good works or penance) can earn our salvation.

We are RECONCILED to God: After Adam and Eve sinned, they were cast out of the Garden of Eden and banished from God's presence. He no longer walked and talked with them as friends. Adam and Eve had fallen out of favor with God who had become their Judge and Adversary. As sinners, all peoples are like foreign nations to God, not worshipping the true God; they are like pagans or Gentiles. When sinners cast themselves on Christ as their only Savior from sin, they are brought near to God in personal fellowship and become one in the family of God (Eph 2:11-18).

We are REDEEMED from Spiritual Bondage: As sinners in rebellion against God, we are enslaved to Satan. We are unable to free ourselves from Satan's dominion. But what we could not do, God did for us. God paid the price to "buy us back" (this is the meaning of "redeemed") through Christ's death on the cross. He "rescued" (or redeemed) us by purchasing us with his blood (Col 1:13-14; Gal 3:13-14; 4:4-7; Eph 2:1-3).

This Salvation Event is what we call CONVERSION: Salvation involves a complete change in the direction of our lives – a "U" turn in our loyalties, affections and desires. It begins with *repentance* wherein a sinner recognizes that he has sinned against God, feels sorrow for that sin, and with humility and a contrite heart cries out for forgiveness. Secondly, conversion includes *faith* – turning to Christ and accepting him as your LORD and SAVIOR.

Conclusion

Salvation can be looked at from different angles. Salvation involves being born again, being justified, being saved from God's wrath and judgment, being reconciled to God with restored fellowship, and being saved from the dominion of Satan and eternal death. Salvation is a "turn around" so that Jesus Christ becomes our Lord and Savior, instead of being enslaved to Satan and under his dominion. This is all by the supernatural and gracious work of the Holy Spirit through faith in Jesus Christ alone.

7. SHARING YOUR FAITH

The waters of Mt. Hermon flow into the Sea of Galilee and then exit into the River Jordan. That Sea is alive with fish. But the Jordan River flows into another Sea with no outlet. Hence it has no life and is the Dead Sea.

Christians are much the same. God calls his children not only to drink deeply from God's Word and thereby grow in the Lord. He calls believers to give out what they have received, to share their faith with others.

Can there be a "secret believer"? God teaches: *"For if you confess with your mouth that Jesus is Lord and believe in your heart that God raised him from the dead, you will be saved. For it is by believing in your heart that you are made right with God, and it is by confessing with your mouth that you are saved"* (Ro 10:9-10).

God calls each of us to share our faith with others. *First, we must demonstrate the Gospel with our lives.* This is basic. If we don't live what we preach, we are mere hypocrites. But the statement of St. Francis of Assisi is fundamentally unbiblical when he allegedly said: "Preach the Gospel, and if necessary, use words." The Gospel should be lived out practically, but a faithful, biblical witness also includes a verbal witness.

Secondly, we should engage in verbal witnessing. This involves developing relationships: praying for our unsaved friends, showing them love and getting to know them by asking questions. Find common ground. Agree where you can agree. Be authentic. Graciously admit your humanity – that you don't know everything, you also have weaknesses. Don't try to force the Gospel on people. Share with them your own testimony, how you came to faith in Christ. Share the Good News of salvation through Christ.

Rebecca (Becky) Manley Pippert and her husband conduct seminars worldwide to help Christians witness in a biblical, Christ-like way. Her resources are very helpful.[iv]

Instead of memorizing an outline and a set of questions, she points to Jesus as our model. Jesus never said the same things with a formulaic approach with everyone, but he met people where they were. Christian witness begins with a Christ-like lifestyle and concern for justice, but it always includes a verbal witness. This witness is built on relationships with sharing your personal testimony of faith in Christ. It is non-confrontational or aggressive. People are turned off by judgmental attitudes. Instead, it is full of questions to learn about the person in his or her situation.

If we have friends who know not Christ, we can share our own testimony of what Jesus means to us and then invite them to a church service where the Gospel is preached.

Many Christians are afraid of witnessing because they feel inadequate. But no one is adequate! Only God can save. We must depend not on our evangelistic skills but on the Holy Spirit who alone can grant the new birth. Christians are frail and incapable of saving, but God is fully able to use our weaknesses and minister through our feeble and faltering efforts.

"What if they ask a question which I cannot answer?" Be authentic. "That's a great question and I'm glad you asked it so I can learn more myself." Don't try to be what you are not – a know-it-all, perfect Christian.

Thirdly, evangelistic tools (methods and means) are made to help Christians who feel inadequate to verbalize their faith. Critics find fault with canned methods, but the fact is that God uses many different means to bring people to Christ. How can anyone complain about a method of evangelism that God is pleased to use to save the lost? *Every* Christian is called upon to bear witness to Jesus Christ who alone can save and memorized methods are useful for many people.

Dr. James Kennedy founded *Evangelistic Explosion* and is famous for two questions you can use with non-Christians.[v] "Have you come to the place in your spiritual life where you can say you know for certain that if you were to die today you would go to heaven?" or/ "Suppose that you were to die today and stand before God and he were to say to you, 'Why should I let you into my heaven?' What would you say?'" The Christian then has the opportunity of explaining the Gospel (Good News) of God's grace to save a lost sinner through the death of Christ.

Bill Bright, founder of Campus Crusade (CRU), came up with a little booklet called, "The Four Spiritual Laws." A Christian can use this if he lacks confidence in sharing the Gospel by himself. God uses many means.

Dr. Mark Olander, an educator in Africa, has written a helpful Teacher's and Student's Manual entitled: "*Disciple Making in the African Church*".[vi] He describes several methods of witnessing in Appendixes: practical suggestions how to share your testimony, using one Bible verse in witnessing (John 3:16 and Romans 6:23), the Bridge Illustration, the "Bad News/Good News Gospel Presentation" and the "Chair Illustration."

8. TRANSFORMING THE MIND

Unbelievers are hostile to God in thinking and depraved in their minds. Hence God has given them over to all kinds of sinful thoughts – selfishness, pride, lust, hatred, greed, dishonesty and deceit (Ro 1:28-32; Col 1:21).

But believers are converted, having repented of their sins and making a "U" turn. They have been set apart for God and throughout their lives they should be growing in holiness. Their minds need to be transformed.

In a most important letter to the Romans, the Apostle Paul lays out the work of Christ in our salvation, beginning with the sinful and unrighteous conduct of humanity, followed by God imputing his righteousness on repentant sinners (justification) and concluding with the growth of believers in holiness (sanctification) (Ro 1:18-8:39). After an interlude on the future of his beloved people, the nation of Israel, he pleads and exhorts:

"Don't copy the behavior and customs of this world, but let God transform you into a new person by changing the way you think" (Ro 12:2).

Sinful behavior springs from sinful thoughts. Avocados don't grow on mango trees. Evil thoughts are the source of sinful deeds (Lk 6:43-45).

Christians have a responsibility to do two things to transform the mind: (1) stop filling the mind with evil thoughts, and (2) keep on filling the mind with God-honoring thoughts.

Stop filling the mind with evil thoughts: God instructs us: *"Above all else, guard your heart, for it affects everything you do"* (Pr 4:23). From the heart spring the words and actions which either glorify God or displease him. Therefore, one of the most important things a Christian can do (*"above all else"*) is to guard what enters into the mind.

The apostle John uses the word, κοσμος (world), with different meanings. A common meaning is that the "world" is evil, something hostile to God. Satan with his fallen angels (evil spirits) play a dominant role in the life of unbelievers through human culture.

Human cultures are created by fallen human beings who are made in God's image but desperately sinful and under the prevailing influence of the spiritual powers of evil. Therefore, a Christian must learn to discern what is Christ honoring in their cultures and what is not. Many, perhaps most of the values enshrined in human culture are evil. John writes:

"Stop loving this evil world and all that it offers you, for when you love the world, you show that you do not have the love of the Father in you.

For the world offers only the <u>lust for physical pleasure</u>, the <u>lust for</u> <u>everything we see</u>, and the <u>pride in our possessions</u>. These are not from the Father. They are from this evil world" (1 Jn 2:15-16).

Much of popular music is sensual. Certain dances can incite sensual feelings. Most TV shows and movies elevate violence, obscenity and sexual pleasures outside of marriage. Watching such programs arouses evil thoughts and makes such conduct seem normal and common place. If God hates such behavior, the Christian should as well. Pleasure for a Christian should never be found in watching sinful behavior. The internet, for all of its benefits, also offers pornography in the privacy of the office. Christians who drink from such cultural cesspools are sinning against God.[vii]

Keep on filling your mind with good thoughts: "Garbage in, garbage out." What goes into the mind, comes out. For Christians to utter godly words and perform godly actions, the mind must continually take in godly thoughts, not ungodly garbage. It's as simple as that.

"Fix your thoughts on what is true and honorable and right. Think about things that are pure and lovely and admirable. Think about things that are excellent and worthy of praise" (Phil 43:8).

For our minds to be transformed into the likeness of Christ, we need to "behold" the glory of the Lord (2 Co 3:18 ESV). *"And we all with unveiled faces, beholding the glory of the Lord, <u>are being transformed into the</u> <u>image from one degree of glory to another</u>. For this comes from the Lord who is the Spirit."*

The Greek word here translated, "beholding," can also mean "reflect as in a mirror." Without extensive explanation, I believe the context supports the idea of "beholding." This is a progressive action. We are not transformed instantly at conversion but gradually by *beholding the glory of the Lord.* This takes place as we read, study, meditate, memorize and reflect on the Word of God prayerfully and in prayerful communion with the Lord.

The mind will never be transformed unless we daily spend time in God's Word and prayerfully seek to understand and obey. We were made in God's image. Our brand new nature given to us at conversion is *"continually being renewed as you learn more and more about Christ"* (Col 3:10).

Christians need to understand: *"This world is not a friend to help us on to God."* Unconsciously, we absorb the values of our culture. Consciously we need to behold the beauty of Christ whose image we are called to reflect.

9. DEVELOPING A CONTRITE, BROKEN HEART

On the one hand, Christians should not sin and need not sin (1 Jn 2:1; Ro 6:1-14). No Christian should blame their sinning on the old sinful nature, for God has provided all we need to resist temptation leading to sin (Eph 6:10-18). We disobey God because we _choose_ to disobey. No excuses.

On the other hand, the tragic truth is that Christians do sin (1 Jn 1:8, 10). God has provided the help we need whenever we sin – an Advocate with the Father and the blood of Christ to cleanse us from our sin (1 Jn 1:9; 2:1f).

However, what is needed before we sin and after we sin is a humility that submissively seeks to please the Lord in all things, and that quickly admits to sinning whenever we fall into sin.

When Adam and Eve were confronted by the Lord about their sin of eating the forbidden fruit, they were defensive and blamed others. When the Lord asked Adam whether he had eaten the forbidden fruit, he replied: "_Yes, but it was the woman you gave me who brought me to the fruit and I ate it_" (Ge 3:12). Adam blamed his wife, but implicitly he blamed God who gave Eve to him. When God inquired of Eve, she blamed her disobedience on the serpent which "tricked" her (Ge 3:13).

Ever since the beginning, people excuse themselves for disobeying the law, blaming other people or their circumstances. Just now I checked the news on the internet and read that a prominent Christian leader in the United States, the President of a large Christian university, _blames others_ for his fall from grace. It is seldom that we find anyone accepting blame until they are forced into a corner. First they lie, then they scape-goat.

King David is an exception. When he lustfully committed adultery with Bathsheba and then heartlessly arranged for her husband to be slain in battle, God sent his prophet, Nathan, to confront David with a clever story of a rich man who stole a lamb from a poor man to feed some guests. David was furious and vowed that the rich man should pay with his life.

"_You are the man!_" Nathan replied. Without hesitation David confessed, "_I have sinned against the LORD_" (2 Sa 12:1-13). Though sin always has consequences, and King David suffered the rest of his life for his grievous sin, God forgave him and he did not die.

We read David's prayer of confession in Psalm 51, a model prayer of confession and repentance. Without hiding from God (a silly thing to do, as Adam and Eve tried), David cried out: "_For I recognize my shameful_ *deeds – they haunt me day and night. Against you, and you alone, have I sinned; I have done what is evil in our sight*" (Ps 51:3-4).

God is not interested in formalities and religious acts of penance. He is not interested in some bland confession, like: "If I have offended you, please forgive me," or "if you have misunderstood me, please forgive me."

Amazingly, David recognizes that God was not primarily interested in burnt offerings and sin offerings. Although God had instituted these sacrifices for God's people to offer when they sin, such formalities are useless and empty without a broken, contrite and humble heart. David replied: "*A broken and repentant heart, O God, you will not despise*" (Ps 51:16).

David was not sinless, but he displayed a humble spirit who was wholly devoted God in seeking to please him. Therefore, God could say of David: "*I have found David son of Jesse a man after my own heart; he will do everything I want him to do*" (Ac 13:33). To live a life pleasing to the Lord means we devote ourselves humbly to serve and obey God, and when we do sin, we humbly acknowledge it, grieve over it, and repent. This requires a humble, broken and contrite heart.

The infinitely great and eternal God, the creator of the heavens and earth, of all things visible and invisible, lives in a high and holy place, ___**and also**___ "*with those whose spirits are contrite and humble*" (Isa 57:15). He further says, "*I will bless those who have humble and contrite hearts, who tremble at my word*" (Isa 66:2). Pause and give thought to these words.

God is God of gods, and Lord of lords. We as Christians are God's creatures, made from the dust of the earth, saved by grace through the atoning work of Christ and wholly dependent on God. If we are truly saved, we must love and obey God with all of our hearts. This takes true humility.

And when we do sin, whether by thought, word or deed, we dare not lie before others, denying that we did it, for God sees all and knows all. We should not commit sin upon sin to defend ourselves. Instead, with humble and contrite hearts we should accept responsibility. "*God sets himself against the proud, but he shows favor to the humble*" (1 Pe 5:5).

Solomon listed seven sins which God hates most. "*A proud look*" is first on the list (Pr 6:16). When I inquired from church leaders in Kenya what were the main reasons Christian leaders fail, *pride* was the first one most often mentioned. Nothing pleases God more than *contrite, broken spirits*.

10. FULFILLING GOD'S PURPOSE FOR YOU

One of the most precious truths in the Bible is that God not only chose each individual in love for himself before the creation of the universe, he created each believer for a particular purpose.

In general the grand purpose of the Christian's life is stated in the first question of the Westminster Shorter Catechism: "*What is the chief end* [purpose or goal] *of man?* "*Man's chief end is to glorify God, and to enjoy him forever*." The goal of each Christian should be to glorify God by thought, word and deed. But this is not some boring, legalistic requirement. Growing in our knowledge of the beauty and majesty of our great God, we find everlasting enjoyment in knowing and living for him.

But God's purpose for each individual is more particular and specific. Each believer is a priceless treasure. Each Christian has meaning and value because God has gifted and prepared each one through life's experiences to do a particular work for him. We are not meaningless blobs that chance has randomly dumped on the earth. Christians are divinely chosen vessels with a particular way in which they were created to glorify God.

One of the most precious verses in the Bible for me is Ephesians 2:10. "*For we are God's masterpiece. He has created us anew in Christ Jesus, so that we can do the good things he planned for us long ago*." Or, as in the ESV: "*We are his workmanship, created in Christ Jesus for good works, which God prepared beforehand, that we should walk in them*."

The paths in which God leads us are not always easy – sickness, pain, death of loved ones, financial struggles, accidents, prodigal children, persecution and other painful disappointments and struggles. *None* of our experiences are wasted, but are used by God to shape us to do "*the good things he planned for us long ago*."

The challenge believers have is to discover God's specific will for their lives and to understand the gifts and abilities with which God has blessed them with in order to bless others. Remember the illustration of the Dead Sea which is lifeless because it only receives the inflow of the Jordan River, but never gives out to refresh the land below it? Christians are blessed when they bless others, but become useless and barren when they do not give out.

This begins with our relationship with the fellowship of believers in a local congregation. God did not save the lost for them to become islands, disconnected from the land. He saved us to become members of the Body of Christ – eyes, mouths, ears, legs, arms, fingers, and toes. SOME Christians are more prominent than others but ALL Christians are important and essential in the functioning of the Body of Christ.

"The eye can never say to the hand, 'I don't need you.' The head can't say to the feet, 'I don't need you.' In fact, some of the parts that seem weakest and least important are really the most necessary" (1 Co 12:21f).

Too many Christians only attend Sunday morning church service, sitting in the back seats and contributing nothing to the Body of Christ. You may think you have nothing to offer, but in fact, if you are truly born again, you have been gifted for a ministry that God ordained you to do long ago.

Such gifts are numerous, for example: cleaning the church, encouraging the sick and suffering, interceding for others in prayer, teaching a Sunday School class, singing in the choir, helping to usher, serving as elders or deacons, counseling the discouraged, and the list goes on. Gifts may need training or cultivating but ***every believer*** is a treasure with gifts and experiences which God has provided for you to use.

Christians, passionate for Christ, should not only use their gifts within the local congregation of believers, they should be passionately committed to being a witness in their community. Differing gifts lead to different opportunities for employment. As you give of your best in employment, you shed the light of the Gospel in both word and deed. Faithful, honest, hardworking, and trustworthy Christians will lessen corruption in society.

"You are the light of the world – like a city on a mountain, glowing in the night for all to see. Don't hide your light under a basket! Instead, put it on a stand and let it shine for all. In the same way, let your good deeds shine out for all to see that everyone will praise your heavenly Father."

Jesus told a parable of a man who gave differing amounts of money (talents) to his servants to invest while he was gone on a journey (Mt 25:14-30). Two of his servants were faithful by investing wisely. Returning from his journey their master was pleased with their faithfulness and rewarded them. But one man who received only one talent failed to invest his money. This resulted in harsh judgment by his master. It is not the kind of gifts that is important, but our faithfulness in using those gifts for God's glory.

All Christians should be much in prayer to seek divine guidance. "What does God want me to do with my life?" The talents/abilities I have are God's gift to me; how I use those gifts is my gift to God.

11. BEING FILLED WITH THE HOLY SPIRIT

Much has been said about what Christians should do to grow as believers and live Christ-honoring lives. But the Bible also teaches that Christians cannot obey and please God apart from being filled with the Spirit.

"So I advise you to live according to your new life in the Holy Spirit. Then you won't be doing what your sinful nature craves...But when the Holy Spirit controls our lives, he will produce this kind of fruit in us: love, joy, peace, patience, kindness, goodness, faithfulness, gentleness, and self-control" (Gal 5:16, 22-23).

Paul taught that those who have been justified by grace through faith in Christ *cannot* keep on sinning as a lifestyle because they "have died to sin" (Ro 6:2). The Apostle John is adamant: *"Those who have been born into God's family do not sin, because God's life is in them. So they can't keep on sinning, because they have been born of God"* (1 Jn 3:9).

The Bible does not teach sinless perfection for the same apostle in the same letter wrote: *"If we say we have no sin, we are only fooling ourselves and refusing to accept the truth"* (1 Jn 1:8). But *"...those who become Christians become new persons. They are not the same anymore, for the old life is gone. A new life has begun!"* (2 "Co 5:17). Their life style changes. What they love and hate changes. They serve different masters.

Paul further states, *"Our old sinful selves were crucified with Christ so that sin might lose its power in our lives. We are no longer slaves to sin"* (Ro 6:6). Since this is true, through the power of the Holy Spirit, Christians should not *"let sin control the way you live; do not give in to its lustful desires. Do not let any part of your body become a tool of wickedness, to be used for sinning. Instead, give yourselves completely to God since you have been given a new life"* (Ro 6:12-13). Paul concludes, *"Now you are free from sin, your old master, and you have become slaves to your new master, righteousness"* (Ro 6:18).

The following chapter (7:1-25) has brought great confusion. Many Christians conclude that Paul is speaking of himself as a Christian in Romans 7 as if he were a slave to sin and unable to keep himself from sinning. This is completely contrary to the teaching of Romans 6.[viii]

Paul shows in Romans 8 that his experience of slavery to sin expressed in Romans 7 was the absence of the Spirit in his life as an unbeliever. Not once in Romans 7 is the Holy Spirit mentioned. In contrast, Paul mentions the Spirit 14 times in Romans 8:1-17. The difference between unbelievers who are "*slaves to sin*" (7:14) and the believers who are "*no longer slaves to sin*" (6::6) is regeneration and the indwelling of the Holy Spirit.

Paul concludes his own personal testimony of failure to keep God's law by asking the question: "*Oh, what a miserable person I am! Who will free me from this life that is dominated by sin? Thank God! The answer is in Jesus Christ our Lord*" (Ro 7:24-25). He continues: "*For the power of the life-giving Spirit has freed you through Christ Jesus from the power of sin that leads to death*" (Ro 8:2). Paul became a new person after conversion.

How clearer could the Bible be? "*God destroyed sin's control over us by giving his Son as a sacrifice for our sins. He did this so that the requirement of the law would be fully accomplished for us who no longer follow our sinful nature but instead follow the Spirit*" (Ro 8:3b-4).

Elsewhere the Bible teaches: "*Don't be drunk with wine…Instead, let the Holy Spirit fill and control you*" (Eph 5:18). The Greek word for "fill" is in the present tense, meaning: "continually be filled." Being filled is not a one-time experience, but an on-going, daily experience of being filled. Every believer is given the Holy Spirit at his new birth. In fact, anyone who does not have the Holy Spirit is *not* a Christian (Ro 8:9).

Being "filled" by the Spirit means "being under control of the Spirit" just as a person drunk with wine is under the control of alcohol.

So how is one continually being filled with the Spirit? Being filled by the Spirit is like breathing: exhaling foul air and breathing in pure oxygen.

Whenever we sin we *grieve* the Holy Spirit, and whenever we disobey the Spirit we *stifle* the Spirit or "*put out the Spirit's fire*" (Eph 4:30; 1 Th 5:19). This means that unconfessed sin prevents us from being filled and controlled by the Spirit. Sin must be continually confessed.

Develop such a great love for God and his Word that your conscience will immediately convict you when you do sin. In humility, with a contrite and broken heart, confess your sin. In this way we breathe out, as it were, the life-threatening carbon dioxide which kills every living organism.

Then we breathe in the life giving fullness of the Holy Spirit. This we do by asking God in faith to fill us with the Spirit to control us. God is ever pleased when we humbly acknowledge our thoughts, words or deeds which do not please God. And God is always eager to fill us with himself to rule in our lives so that we reflect the beauty of our great Savior.

12. RUNNING LIFE'S MARATHON TO WIN THE RACE

Life is like a marathon – a life-long race with many hurdles. It is good for Christians to live their whole lives with the end goal in mind, to win the race. How then should we live? How should an athlete run a race? Athletes run with the end of the race in mind – winning the trophy.

Young people may think they have a long life ahead of them, but beware! Life is very short. I well remember arriving at Scott Theological College at the age of 30, thrilled to be there after first being called by God to serve in Africa as a missionary fifteen years earlier. Missionaries gathered for days of prayer. Looking at the older missionaries with grey hair, I literally thought to myself: "You poor old missionaries. You only have a few years left, but I have a whole life to serve here." But in only a short time I became another "old missionary" ready for retirement.

The Greeks held four Panhellenic athletic games including the Olympic Games, the most famous, as well as the Isthmian Games which were located outside the city of Corinth. Most likely Paul attended a number of those games for he used athletics to illustrate the Christian life. He declares that Christians should live their lives as if they were in a race to win. Instead of doing the least that is necessary to be Christian, each Christian should *"run in such a way that you will win,"* knowing that only one receives a prize (1 Co 9:24-27).

Our race in life is *not* a short sprint but a life-long marathon. Many Christians start their race well. But as we all know, the winner is not necessarily the one who outpaces the others at first. The winner perseveres with pains and aches, and pushes on to the end.

All kinds of troubles are encountered in life including persecution. Being mocked or ridiculed by peers is the least of our problems. Worse than that, new Christians may be cast out of their homes or ostracized from their community. Beatings and imprisonment are common in certain countries.

Lesser problems include sickness, death in the family, financial struggles, disputes in families and employment. In this world, problems are endless.

Nothing takes place in the lives of Christians without God, lovingly and with a good purpose, ordaining it to happen. Peter explains the purpose:

"These trials are only to test your faith, to show that it is strong and pure. It is being tested as fire tests and purifies gold – and your faith is far more precious to God than mere gold. So if your faith remains strong after being

tried by fiery trials, it will bring you much praise and glory and honor on the day when Jesus Christ is revealed to the whole world" (1 Pe 1:7).

Paul rejoiced in his suffering because he knew that they would cause him to grow and become more Christ-like (Ro 5:1-4). James counsels the Christians to "*count it all joy…when you meet trials of various kinds*" because "*the testing of your faith produces steadfastness…that you may be perfect and complete, lacking nothing*" (Ja 1:2 ESV). Winning life's marathon race requires perseverance and steadfastness despite suffering, because suffering builds steadfastness into a Christian's character.

The writer of Hebrews uses the same metaphor of racing (Heb 12:1-2). Having described the heroes of faith in Hebrews 11, he imagines them, after winning their races, sitting in the amphitheater's seats and cheering:

"*Therefore, since we are surrounded by such a huge crowd of witnesses to the life of faith, let us strip off every weight that slows us down, especially the sin that so easily hinders our progress. And let us run with endurance the race that God has set before us. **We do this by keeping our eyes on Jesus**, on whom our faith depends from start to finish.*"

That is the key: throwing off anything that hinders you from winning and keeping your eyes on Jesus, not the problems – "*who for the joy that was set before him endured the cross, despising the shame, and is seated at the right hand of the throne of God*" (Heb 12:2 ESV).

The beginning of failure in the lives of Christians or church leaders is not some spectacular fiasco that becomes public and leads to their downfall. The beginning of their failure is the neglect of basic spiritual disciplines described in the previous chapter – failure to cultivate a close relationship with the Lord. The big failure is the result of slowly and unperceptively drifting away from their first love of the Lord. The warning found in Hebrews is prescient: "*So we must listen very carefully to the truth we have heard, or we may drift away from it*" (Heb 2:1).

Lessons learned from athletics are instructive for the race of life.

"*You must run in such a way that you will win. All athletes practice strict self-control. They do it to win a prize that will fade away, but we do it for an eternal prize. So I run straight to the goal with purpose in every step. I am not like a boxer who misses his punches. I discipline my body like an athlete, training to do what it should. Otherwise, I fear that after preaching to others, I myself might be disqualified*" (1 Co 9:24b-27).

CONCLUSION

The thought of solving the problem of corruption in the church or in the nation is daunting. Such a challenge is so overwhelming that one is tempted to give up without even trying, until you consider two truths.

First, Christians cannot solve the problem of corruption either within the Church or in any nation. Only God can. The problem is sinful hearts and only God can transform the heart. But is anything too hard for God? Is God limited? Is God uninterested in his Church being holy, loving and Christ-like? Of course we know the answer. God desires his people, saved by grace, to be renewed into the likeness of Christ. God is able!

Second, God asks Christians to solve the corruption problem in their own hearts. If you as an individual Christian in your family, local congregation and community embrace the building blocks laid out in this book, your life will be changed. Implicitly, your relationships with others in your sphere of living will be transformed. As likeminded Christians gather together for persistent and faithful prayers for spiritual renewal in your local congregation, lives will be changed one by one. God is able.

In the United States material prosperity and wealth turned many away from God in the mid-1850s. Cynicism and unbelief ran deep in America when William Miller, a forerunner of the S.D.A., predicted the return of Christ in 1844 and this failed to happen. The love of many turned cold.

"God in his divine grace began to stir the hearts of many to pray for revival. Jeremiah Lamphier started a prayer meeting in New York City in September 1857 in a Dutch Reformed Church. Six people came the first week, increasing the next week to 14 and then 23. They decided to meet every day for prayer and began to fill the churches, first the Dutch Reformed Church, the Methodist Church and then the Episcopal Church. These prayer meetings continued to grow until over 10,000 men were meeting daily for prayer in New York City."[ix]

Gradually this spread throughout the nation until one million were converted in America and one million in the United Kingdom.

Revival is from God and comes in his timing and by his sovereign grace. Christians cannot manipulate God or program revival. But Christians are surely called upon to humble themselves and with contrite, broken hearts call upon God to renew their own lives and their own church and nation.

Part Two: Leadership Development

Believers are compared to sheep in the Bible who need a shepherd. Sheep are notoriously dumb. They wander off and become lost, or follow a lead-sheep to the slaughter. They allegedly even walk over a cliff if led. As the Bible teaches: *"All of us have strayed away like sheep. We have left God's paths to follow our own…"* (Isa 54:6).

Therefore, sheep need a shepherd to lead them and feed them, to protect them and seek the lost. Unlike western and African shepherds who "lead" from behind by pushing the sheep forward, the oriental shepherd leads from the front. When the "Good Shepherd" calls each sheep by name, *"he goes before them, and the sheep follow him, for they know his voice"* (Jn 10:4).

For the believer the Chief Shepherd is the LORD God himself (Ps 23). Our loving God leads his own sheep to green pastures to refresh them. He leads them beside "still waters" which do not frighten them, but quenches their thirst, and he leads them in "paths of righteousness." He comforts and protects the sheep during life-threatening experiences. His very presence is reassuring for he wields a club and staff to protect and rescue them.

The LORD shepherds his flock by using under-shepherds to feed, lead and protect his sheep. But alas, many of these under-shepherds in the Old Testament were "self-centered." They failed to take care of God's sheep. So God spoke through Ezekiel to denounce these shepherd-leaders.

"Son of man, prophesy against the shepherds, the leaders of Israel. Give them this message from the Sovereign LORD. Destruction is certain for you shepherds who feed yourselves instead of your flocks. Shouldn't shepherds feed their sheep? You drink the milk, wear the wool, and butcher the best animals, but you let your flocks starve. You have not taken care of the weak. You have not tended the sick or bound up the broken bones…Instead, you have ruled them with force and cruelty. So my sheep have been scattered without a shepherd. They are easy prey for any wild animal…You took care of yourselves and left the sheep to starve…I now consider these shepherds my enemies, and I will hold them responsible for what has happened to my flock" (Eze 34:2-10).

In Part One of this chapter we spoke of twelve building blocks that individual Christians need to follow in order for them to become mature, vibrant Christians. When enough Christians in a local congregation embody those twelve building blocks, that local congregation becomes a dazzling light and witness in their society.

But one building block is missing – the need for faithful and godly shepherd-leaders. Sheep need shepherds just as babies need mothers. In this Part Two we begin with the qualifications of Christian shepherds.

In brief, the two basic qualifications for Christian shepherds are these: *character* and *competency*. They need to know God and *reflect godly character*, and they need to know *how to lead, feed, and protect* their flock.

In these few pages we cannot provide the necessary help for the training of Christian leaders, but we will stress the need for *godly character* and *experienced competency* to shepherd God's flock. Suggestions for further reading and more comprehensive assistance are hereby provided.[x]

CHARACTER AND COMPTENCY

A few years before our retirement in 2002 I felt led to visit and interview 170 of our Scott graduates. Among my many questions, I asked: "Why do church leaders succeed?" and "Why do they fail?"

What struck me was that in their opinion, by far the greatest reason church leaders fail was failed character. Their failure was not primarily because they could not deliver an edifying sermon, or evangelize the lost or counsel a troubled parishioner. They failed because of character flaws. These failed church leaders had not guarded their hearts, nor had they nourished their souls with God's Word and prayer. Consequently, they fell into the lust of the flesh (usually, adultery), lust of the eyes (often misappropriation of funds) or pride of life (egotism manifested by a "big man" mentality with jealousy of any threat to their position). See 1 John 5:15-17.[xi]

Character

Before church leaders are chosen, they should pass a character test. A good place to start is by examining the qualifications for elders/bishops laid out in Scripture (1 Ti 3:1-13; Tit 1:5-9; 1 Pe 5:1-4).

First, the prospective deacon, elder, pastor, bishop or chairman must be a mature, experienced person of a good reputation, someone who has grown spiritually by embracing the twelve building blocks that all Christians should embrace as found in Part One of this chapter.

As the Apostle Paul stated: *"An elder must not be a new Christian because he might be proud of being chosen so soon and the Devil will use that pride to make him fall."* Further, *"For an elder must be a man whose life cannot be spoken against."* Paul lists other qualifications: *"faithful to his wife,"* having *"a good reputation," "he must be gentle, peace loving, and not one who loves money"* etc. (1 Ti 3:1-7).

Christians often receive the leaders they deserve. When choosing church leaders, too many Christians choose those who are related to their family and clan, or those who are prominent men in the community, irrespective of their failure to measure up to the spiritual qualifications of Scripture.

The end result is failure and worse. When these leaders fall into sinful behavior, they disgrace and shame God and his Church.

Every congregation should be in prayer as they carefully examine the lives of those they choose for leadership. The leaders will either bless the congregation with servant-leadership, or they will trouble the congregation with unwise, unfaithful and unspiritual leadership.

Competency

Godly character is by far the most important qualification for church leaders. Charismatic leadership can *never* replace godly character.

However, no church leader is perfect. What is most important is a broken and contrite heart. If leaders lose their temper, or say unkind words or in some other way fall short of God's perfect standard, they need a spirit of humility to readily and quickly acknowledge, confess and repent publicly when that sin has occurred publicly or privately to individuals offended.

But effective church leaders need more than mature, godly character. They need competency in ministerial skills including: preaching, teaching, discipling, evangelizing, counseling and peoples skills.

No Christian leader, however, has all these gifts in full measure. Some are more gifted in evangelism than in preaching, or they are better with interpersonal relationship skills than in teaching. Members need patience and understanding with church leaders who may not be measure up to their likes in one area or another. But all ministers of the Gospel need some measure of skills in all these areas.

I have seen effective church leaders who disappoint and frustrate me in their preaching, but whose interpersonal relationship skills endeared them to the congregation and helped build up the church. We need to understand the limitations of church leaders, and love them and respect them as they are, as long as they are godly and faithful.

Remember, in Scripture a church leader is considered a shepherd who cares for the flock of sheep. They provide all that the sheep needs. The apostle Peter identified himself as an "elder" and appealed to his "fellow elders" in this way: "_Care_ for the flock of God entrusted to you" (1 Pe 5:2). More literally it reads: "_Shepherd_ the flock…" (ESV). Sheep need to be fed, led and protected, and shepherds do this by preaching, teaching, discipling, evangelizing, and ministering to them on a personal level.

Inter-personal Relationship (Peoples) Skills: Paul taught that an elder "_must enjoy having guests in his home_" (1 Ti 3:2). This qualification refers to a sociable, friendly, loving and caring person.

The elder/pastor/bishop needs to minister to people in their homes apart from official church services. He needs to visit the Christians in their homes, learn of their problems and struggles, teach them the Word of God and pray with them. This is _most_ important for an oral society. Most literate Africans are still oral people who benefit greatly by personal attention and person-to-person ministry of the spoken word.

Christians face many challenges. Couples may have marriage problems, parents may have prodigal children, and young people may struggle with unwise or ungodly choices. Elders/pastors/bishops need to understand how to talk with them confidentially and provide sound counsel. This requires a knowledge of Scripture and sound training in counseling skills.

Preaching and Teaching: This is a skill that requires much training to know the Scriptures and know how to present the Word of God effectively. Without biblical preaching and teaching, the sheep will remain infants in their walk with the Lord. They also will be gullible and misled into heresy.

All kinds of false teaching abounds, teaching that contains half-truths and partial truths. This can be confusing to the untaught Christian because the false teacher quotes the Scripture to prove his point. We need to teach the flock under our care so that they are not misled by false teaching.

Evangelizing and Discipling: No church can be Christ-centered, nor can it grow unless both pastor and his flock are actively seeking the lost. This means that the pastor must have a vibrant Christian testimony and know how to lead the unsaved to faith in Christ. This task of evangelism belongs to all members of the flock, but the flock must be taught and trained by the pastor to become active witnesses in their families and communities. Evangelism never stands alone. New converts need to be grounded in the faith. They need to be taught the Word of God and the spiritual disciplines.

TRAINING

If we are to solve corruption in the nation and church, all elders, deacons, evangelists, pastors, and bishops need training that is appropriate for their sphere of ministry. If the bishops and chairmen, who oversee pastors and local congregations, are serious about growing and strengthening their under-shepherds, the training of elders and pastors must be a priority!!!

This should be self-evident from what has already been said. Knowing, understanding and applying the Word of God to the personal lives of every Christian is _absolutely_ essential for growing baby Christians into mature, godly Christians. This training must not be merely academic but spiritual; not merely knowing the truths of Scripture, but applying them to the lives of Christians by the work of the Holy Spirit.

The elders and pastors who preach and teach the flock need training in the skills of preaching (homiletics) and teaching, counseling and the duties of the pastoral ministry.

Given the various contexts where little congregations of believers are found, this can be a challenge. But the most basic issue is whether the bishops and overseers of pastors recognize the importance of this and are committed to it! _Solving the corruption in the church and nation is not possible without the holistic training of deacons, elders, pastors, evangelists and bishops_. By "holistic training" we mean exactly what has been said: a basic understanding of Scripture and theology, and a knowledge of how to preach, teach, evangelize, disciple, and counsel the people under their care, with the formation of godly character.

Training is no substitute for a godly character. Many _highly educated_ church leaders have gone astray because they have neglected the nurturing of their relationship with Christ. Education itself is _not_ the panacea for the spiritual problems in the church. But appropriate training in the knowledge of Scripture and theology together with training and experience in the skills of church ministry are essential for an effective ministry.

Training of Elders

Let's begin with the leadership of elders. In biblically minded churches the elders play a vital role in ministry. They are the overseers of the flock in the local congregation. In many contexts in Africa they serve as on-site untrained pastor-shepherds of the local church.

In large churches, especially in the urban centers, they have multiple full-time, well supported pastors along with elders. But in smaller churches, as we read in the New Testament, they only have unpaid lay Christians who serve as the teaching-shepherds of the flock.

The multi-church-pastors shepherd many small congregations, sometimes up to 12 or more. In practice the elders of these smaller churches must preach and lead worship every Sunday and care for the flock in the absence of the trained pastor overseeing them. Only once a month or once a quarter does the pastor-in-charge preach in each church.

In these cases a conscientious, faithful pastor must make it his primary ministry to _train_ these elders so that they know the Scriptures and be able to preach and teach the little flock in his absence. Possibilities include:

Theological Education by Extension (TEE): The Association of Evangelicals of Africa took over the TEXT-Africa project started by Rev. Fred Holland. Under the A.E.A., teams of missionaries and Africans worked together to prepare some thirty books on biblical studies and topical studies such as prayer, marriage and evangelism. Each book is designed to cover ten weeks with five lessons each week. These books are intended to be "the teacher" with its programmed formatting. The leader facilitates discussion after the students answer the questions in the 200 page books.

The purpose of TEXT-Africa project is to train students for ministry, especially lay Christians, without needing to leave work and join a residential school. The older, more mature persons who are married and employed are the target individuals who are already active in ministry.

The weakness of the TEXT-Africa project is that the "curriculum" is not designed to provide a terminus for the completion of the course. No one can say when a student can "graduate." It also lacks studies on theology and pastoral skills. A financial challenge is the need for the pastor to purchase the books and then sell them to the students. Further, some pastors see TEE as extra work for which there is no remuneration.

"The Multi-Church Pastor: A Manual for Training Leadership in a Multi-Church Situation" by Philip E. Morrison is a practical manual that supplements one aspect missing in TEXT-Africa project. Morrison had been a pastor in the United States for many years, then taught in Moffat

College of the Bible in Kenya for ten years where he discovered the plight of many smaller Kenyan churches which are led by untrained elders much of the time. Bible School/College students may be well trained, but unprepared to serve as a multi-church pastor. He found no help for the multi-church pastor to train the elders.

This launched him into the preparation of a 113 page book, "*The Multi-Church Pastor*," which has been field-tested and taught in numerous Bible Schools and at pastors' conferences. This training manual with its interactive curriculum trains elders to preach, plan and lead worship, do visitation and counseling. [xii]

Bible Training Centre for Pastors (BTCP/L): Ten courses with manuals are designed to provide basic training for shepherding a local congregation. Courses include: Bible Study Methods and Rules of Interpretation; Old Testament and New Testament Surveys, Preaching Bible Messages, Bible Doctrine Survey, Personal Spiritual Life, Church Ministry – Administration and Education; Teaching Principles and Methods; Church History Survey; and Missions, Evangelism, Discipleship.

Student motivation comes from personal desire to become equipped for church ministry. No tests are given. Though BTCP/L is used worldwide in 100 countries, "African Leadership" networks with Country Directors. Nearly 40,000 pastors, church leaders and community leaders have graduated from the two year course by 2019.

Commitment of Denominational Leadership: These are the only three available training programs at this time specifically designed to train African church elders. By one way or another, however, church elders, who lead worship and preach on Sundays and serve practically as the shepherds of a local congregation, need training. Let me repeat!! If elders are expected to preach and lead in worship on Sunday mornings, and if they are for all practical purposes the on-sight shepherds to lead, feed and protect the sheep, *elders need training*.

A common saying is: "Where there is a will, there is a way." Although that is unbiblical strictly speaking (only with God's favor and help can we do anything), there is an element of truth in this. Challenges are many to train all the elders in multi-church pastoral situations, but it is doable if the leadership is committed. If the leadership sees this as a need, with God's help, they can make it happen. And without the training, the sheep will remain infantile in their spiritual lives and easily distracted and led astray.

Training of Evangelists, Pastors and Bishops

The level and amount of training needed for evangelists, pastors and bishops depends on their intended focus of ministry. More education is not necessarily the best answer. Many students become professional students, lifting them to levels that are impractical for their context of ministry.

For example, training a pastor from the nomadic, pastoral societies in northern Kenya in Bible Colleges located in the educationally advanced southern Kenya is not practical. Their education is not contextualized and it acclimates the students to conveniences and comforts not available in the arid north. On the other hand, lower levels of education may not be adequate for pastoring an urban church with highly educated parishioners.

Tragically, a major problem of jealousy often prevails among the lower levels of educated pastors against the more highly educated pastors. Such jealousy is very real and seriously hinders church growth. If only church leaders could accept who they are, and the gifts and training they have received, and humbly serve without jealously striving to prevent others from being chosen to take their place!!!

Circumstances differ. The important issue is that sheep cannot be led, fed, and protected without trained leadership. Knowledge and application of the Word of God is pivotal for growing in Christ. Without a deepening relationship with the Lord through the Word of God and prayer, the sheep will be malnourished. This results in carnality and worldliness, corrupting the church and nation.

Various kinds of church leadership training are available in Africa. Residential schooling at various academic levels is most common, including one or two year Bible Training Centers, diploma level courses, first degree and advanced degree courses. Residential training is of great value if that is possible because a student not only learns in the classroom, but from other students, informal interactions with teachers and practical field education. Its limitation is cost and the need to leave employment.

Apprenticeship or on-the-job training is a very practical and traditional way of learning. Instead of being immersed in abstract, theoretical concepts of ministry, students learn by serving under an experienced church leader. Learning on the job should be augmented by supervised book learning of Bible, theology and other topics. A trained pastor could ideally be given the responsibility to mentor, teach and supervise the in-service student.

Those with access to the internet and a computer can find many Bible and theological courses available on-line.

Specialized training is available designed specifically to train an evangelist or a missionary. Cross cultural ministry requires studies not normally found in Bible Schools which are designed to train pastors.

Before all other considerations, the most fundamental question is this: What is my calling? To whom is God calling me to serve? With that in mind, prayerfully and wisely consider your options. Take one step at a time.

Hopefully, the leaders in your denomination will have options for you to consider. You need *both* a knowledge of Scripture and theology, *and* competency in the skills of ministry. When learning in a residential situation or under the care of an experienced mentor-pastor, provision will hopefully be made for spiritual formation as well – the learning of spiritual disciplines to keep you growing and guarding you from failing.

END NOTES

[i] The *Africa Study Bible*, published by Oasis International Ltd., has 2.400 features, written by hundreds of African Ph.D. level scholars from 45 countries. Its purpose is to help African Christians grow in their Christian faith through understanding the Holy Scriptures from an African perspective. It is a treasure worth far more than the money needed to buy.

[ii] These five questions with explanations are found in *"In It to Win It"* © 1992, 2013 by Steve Lawson, published by Harvest House Pub.

[iii] *Overcoming Fear of Death"* (published by Oasis International and copyrighted by Richard J. Gehman) was written to help overcome the fear of death by understanding and embracing the biblical truth of salvation. Also read: *Saved Without a Doubt* and *The Gospel According to Jesus* by John MacArthur; *Finally Alive* by John Piper.

[iv] Rebecca Pippert wrote a book thirty years ago, selling millions of copies, which is relevant today, called: *Out of the Salt Shaker and into the World*." She has written many books to help Christians learn how to witness and how to lead unbelievers in Seeker Bible Studies. Her web site is: <beckypippert.com>. You will find many resources highly recommended.

[v] Read Wikipedia's article and footnotes on *Evangelism Explosion*.

[vi] *Disciple Making in the African Church* by Mark Olander, published by Oasis.

[vii] Pornography has been available for decades, but with the advent of the internet, pornography is obtainable anywhere that the internet is

accessible. Through the cell phone Africans have access to 100 porn sites where 28 billion people in the world visit yearly. South Africa is among the top 20 countries in the world that watch pornography the most. It ranks 2nd in the world for time spent per visit on porn sites.

Pornography is a mortal threat to individuals, marriages and nations. It increases the odds of teenage pregnancy, increases depression with feelings of loneliness. It creates distorted expectations which hinder a healthy view of sex. Use of pornography increases marital infidelity by 300%. 56% of divorces in the U.S.A. report one partner with "obsessive interest" in pornography. Porn robs the nations of students and workers who should be focused on their work and studies but are drawn to pornography. Catching a few minutes of porn can easily be done without people knowing it.

And most important, pornography is sinful because "*anyone who even looks at a woman with lust in his eye has already committed adultery with her in his heart*" (Mt 5:28). Porn is addictive. You see a little and you want more. Porn distorts the value of women and turns them into "sport" or property. It reduces them to attractive bodies without reference to their hearts, minds, gifts, personality or relationship with Jesus Christ.

For a Christian, porn should be avoided like the plague.

[viii] Paul calls himself "unspiritual, sold as a slave to sin" (7:14). He claims that he desires to do good, but cannot (7:18); that he is "captive to the law of sin and death" (7:23). Paul's use of the present tense in 7:13-23 surely seems to imply that Paul's slavery to sin was a present reality as a believer. But this is contrary to what he teaches in 6:10ff.

The solution to this conundrum is the fact that the Greek present tense, just like in the English language, can be used in either a futuristic or historical sense. Elsewhere the King James translates the Greek present tense with the English present tense (Mk 14:17 "*he cometh*"; Mt 3:1 "*preaching in the wilderness*"; Jn 1:29 "*John seeth Jesus*"), but the ESV correctly translates the sense of the Greek present as a past tense.

Hence, we conclude that to reconcile the apparent contradiction between Paul's teaching in Romans 6 with his own experience in Romans 7, we must understand Paul's personal testimony as an historical account of his failed effort as a pious Jew to obey the law before his conversion. His own past experience is told in the present tense for dramatic effect, even as we today frequently use the present tense in English to describe a past experience for dramatic effect.

[ix] *The Roots of Christianity in Africa*" prepared by the TAG Research Team on prayer, published 1989, available at Scott Christian University.

[x] A few selected books on leadership include:
Adeyemo, Tokunboh. *The Making of a Servant of God*.
Barber, Cyril. *Nehemiah and the Dynamics of Effective Leadership*.
Clinton, Robert. *The Making of a Leader*.
Eims, LeRoy. *Be the Leader You Were Meant to Be*.
Engstrom, Ted. *The Making of a Christian Leader*.
Finzel, Hans. *The Top Ten Mistakes Leaders Make*.
Gangel, Kenneth. *Competent to Lead*.
Gehman, Richard. *Learning to Lead*.
Gitari, David. *Responsible Leadership*.
Janvier, George and Bitrus Thaba. *Understanding Leadership: An African Christian Model*.
Kapena, Sumbye. *How to be a Wise Leader*.
Kohls, Paul. "A Look at Church Leadership in Africa," AJET No 2: 107f.
Love, J. Richard. *Liberating Leaders from the Superman Syndrome*.
Mbogori, Elijah. *Conflict Management*.
Osei-Mensah, Gottfried. *Wanted: Servant Leaders*.
Richards, and Clyde Hoeldtke. *A Theology of Church Leadership*.
Sanders, J. Oswald. *Spiritual Leadership*.
Stott, John. *Basic Christian Leadership*.
Stowell, Joseph M. *Shepherding the Church*.

[xi] *Learning to Lead: The Making of a Christian Leader in Africa* by Richard J. Gehman. This is a 335 page textbook that reflects extensive interviews with 170 church leaders who graduated from Scott Theological College. Copyrighted and first published by Oasis in 2008. *The Secret of Success for Christian leaders in Africa* is a shortened version of that book with 85 pages.

[xii] Philip Morrison's books are published by OASIS and are both helpful and relevant for all African church leaders. They are pithy and to the point.

Morrison, Philip E. *Conflict Resolution in the Church*.
Morrison, Philip E. *Influence: Leading Without Position*.
Morrison, Philip E. *Seven Surprises for the Pastor*.
Morrison, Philip E. *Stewardship of Time*.
Morrison, Philip E. *Questions Pastors Ask*.

OASIS INTERNATIONAL
Satisfying Africa's Thirst for God's Word

Our mission is to grow discipleship through publishing African voices.
Go to oasisinternationalpublishing.com to learn more.

INFLUENCE: LEADING WITHOUT POSITION
Philip E. Morrison & Hankuri Tawus Gaya
Do you have ideas for how to change your community, church, or nation – but feel powerless to make them happen? This book tells you how you can influence others to take action and start change, just as young men and women in the Bible did.

HIGHLY FAVOURED: OUR POWERFUL GOD'S COVENANT WITH YOU
Stuart J. Foster
The God of the Bible is not unreliable or inaccessible like the spiritual beings in African traditional religions. He chooses to have a covenant relationship with his people and we do not have to earn God's favour.

AFRICANS AND AFRICA IN THE BIBLE
Tim Welch
This book shows the presence and the participation of Africans in the biblical text, helping demonstrate that Christianity is not a "white man's religion" and that Christianity has deep roots in African soil.

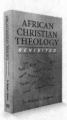

AFRICAN CHRISTIAN THEOLOGY REVISITED
Richard J. Gehman
For all African Christians, *African Christian Theology Revisited* is a powerful plea to think through your faith in African contexts under the authority of the Word of God.

RAISING UP GOOD STEWARDS
Joseph William Black
For anyone who leads a church, a ministry, or an organization in Africa, *Raising Up Good Stewards* gives practical solutions for ministry. Learn how to increase church giving with integrity, support your family and the needy, and restore the church's witness, and credibility in corrupt contexts.

HELPING WITHOUT HURTING IN AFRICA
Jonny Kabiswa Kyazze and Anthony Sytsma with Brian Fikkert
This book trains leaders to proclaim the gospel in both word and deed, changing mind-sets and helping them apply biblical principles to care wisely and compassionately for people who are poor without unintentionally doing harm.

LEARNING TO LEAD
Richard J. Gehman
With its discussion questions and practical applications, this book will guide you to obtaining character and skills and help you become an effective Christian leader. It was written from the living experience of African leaders and it has been shaped by 36 years of training church leaders in Kenya.

ANSWERS FOR YOUR MARRIAGE
Bruce and Carol Britten
Offers practical insights to marriage issues and facts on sex, pregnancy, family planning, child-raising, money issues, adultery, HIV, and sex-related diseases. If your marriage is in despair, look to this book for some answers for your marriage.

PARENTING WITH PURPOSE & AFRICAN WISDOM
Gladys K. Mwiti
This practical guide for Christians is a relevant, thoughtful presentation on the characteristics of parenting that delivers results.

THE RADICAL MONEY MANIFESTO
Joseph William Black
Based on the biblical and church history insights of *Raising Up Good Stewards*, *The Radical Money Manifesto* includes Bible study questions for learning to be stewards together. Jesus offers freedom from fretting, justice for the poor, and investment opportunities with eternal pay-offs. Whatever it costs, Jesus promises it will be worth it.

OASIS INTERNATIONAL PUBLISHING

oasisinternationalpublishing.com | oasisinternational.com